G STREET CHRONICLES PRESENTS

EXECUTIVE *Mistress*

written by

George Sherman Hudson

&

Mz. Robinson

Published by:
G Street Chronicles
P.O. Box 490082
College Park, GA 30349

www.gstreetchronicles.com
Fan@gstreetchronicles.com

This is a work of fiction. It is not meant to depict, portray or represent any particular real person. All the characters, incidents, and dialogues are the products of the author's imagination and are not to be construed as real. Any references or similarities to actual events, entities, real people, living or dead, or to real locales are intended to give the novel a sense of reality. Any similarity in other names, characters, entities, places, and incidents is entirely coincidental.

Cover Design: Vonda Howard, Cupcake Creative Studios
vondahoward@me.com
Typesetting: Shawna A Grundy,
sag@shawnagrundy.com

LCCN: 2010934534
ISBN: 978-0-9826543-5-4

Join us on Facebook G Street Chronicles Fan Page

EXECUTIVE *Mistress*

George Sherman Hudson

I want to thank God for giving me the strength to make this happen.

To all my family & friends - I want to thank yall for all your love and support.

To my special friend, Shawna A. Grundy - Thanks for holding me down…we're just gettin' started.

To my right hand, Marcel - I appreciate what you do. Keep up the hard work. We're gonna see seven figures in a minute.

I want to thank all the people out there who continue to support me and *G Street Chronicles*. And to all the authors that rep *G Street*, Queen B.G., India, Mz. Robinson, Joe Awsum, Cole Hart, Khaream, and my good friend Charlene Davis.

This book is dedicated
to all the executives out there with a mistress.
Keep it playa

To my Lord and Savior, I am grateful that you allowed me to stumble and fall, for without doing so I would not know what it is to be humble and how to truly count each and every one of my blessings. Thank you for picking me up and renewing my blessings every morning. I am nothing without you.

To my parents: Ray and Shirley the two of you are the best parents anyone could ask for. Thank you for making me laugh, listening to my problems time and time again, standing by me no matter what, and never saying, " I told you so." I love you both and I am honored to be your daughter.

To Banita Brooks, my bestie who has been there for me like a blood sister. Banita, I will never forget when my " money was looking funny" you had my back. That's real and you are a true friend who I will ride with till the end. I love you sis.

To my uncle Kenneth Leslie, you are always a phone call away and when you say you're coming or going to get it done, you do. I love how you keep it real no matter what. Thank you "Uncle Bay", I love you.

To my uncle Michael Leslie, I still can't say thank you enough for what you did. I love you.

To Valerie Ann Williams, thank you for supporting me, spreading the word, and all the fabulous get togethers. Love ya Val.

To Doris, thank you for supporting me, spreading the word, and staying on me about these books. Love ya.

To Vonda Howard, you already know, thank you for another hot cover. To Autumn, my editor, thank you.

To all the readers, fans, reviewers, and authors who show me love, thank you!

To K. J., the G, the gentleman, and my homie for life. Thank you for encouraging me, always being happy for me, and for making me laugh. I know at times it seems like I'm too busy to even pick up the phone but know I am here for you and the friendship is and always has been real.

Last but not least to my publisher George Sherman Hudson, thank you for the opportunity to work with you and for the support. We've had our ups and downs (due to your failure to realize I was right and you were wrong. (Laughs and smiles) but you have been there like family and I thank you for that. Love and Respect Always.

To all those dreaming of bigger and better things, speak it into existence and doubt not.

~Kisses,

Mz. R

Mz. Robinson

I would like to dedicate this book
in memory of
my Grandmother, Earlean Turner Leslie.
Although, she is gone, she will never-ever be forgotten.

Ma-Ma, I still remember the last time I saw you and the sadness I felt in my young heart from knowing that God was preparing to call you home. You were a beautiful and strong woman that I am truly honored to have known. I know if you were here today you would smile at what I've accomplished and probably shake your head at some of the decisions I have made. However, I know you would still love and support me no matter what. I take pleasure in knowing you are resting peacefully and one day we will meet again. I love you and my memories of you are forever inked in my heart.

Chapter 1

"Asia Turner!"

The sound of my name blasting over the intercom made me sigh with relief, first because the gnawing silence in the room had been broken and second because my ass was numb from sitting for over two hours straight. Although the executive conference room was packed with over a hundred job-hungry applicants waiting for their chance, until my name was called the room had been so quiet you could hear a roach fart.

"Good luck," the perky blonde sitting next to me said as I rose from my chair.

I gave her a brief smile, then exited the room. I wanted to tell her I didn't need luck; I had a BA from the prestigious Howard University, recommendations from some of the most prominent state officials in Alabama, and my I-can't-be-stopped attitude. I knew the position was mine. I walked through the open door of the human resources office with my head held high, smiling like a woman who had just won the Power Ball lottery.

Walking up to the desk, I extended my hand to the

heavyset woman who was staring at me. Her eyes went from my face down to my above-the-knee skirt, then back up again. "Have a seat," she said, leaving me hanging.

I reluctantly dropped my hand and did as the woman instructed.

"I'm Elena Toney, Human Resources Manager here at G&L," she recited as if she were reading an imaginary script. "I've reviewed your resume and credentials, and although they are impressive, I'm sure you know there are other candidates here whose accomplishments exceed your little achievements."

What the fuck? I thought as I listened in silence, visualizing running her fat ass down with a Mack truck! It was obvious the woman was a miserable, hating bitch! Regardless, I was not feeling the way she was coming at me.

"That said," she continued, "why you?"

I smiled sweetly. "Ms. Toney, you are correct. G& L can choose any one of the other candidates to fill this position, but why not choose the best? Not only can I do this job, but I'll do it well. During my summer internship with Elise Inc., I secured five contracts, and—"

"That may be true," Elena cut me off, "but here at G&L, our representatives land over five contracts a day." She shook her head and laughed. "Miss Turner, let me give you a little advice." She leaned forward in her chair. "You have to crawl before you can walk. Maybe you should start off small, go back to Elise and reapply. Unless, there is a reason you can't go back." She eyed me suspiciously, causing my blood to boil slowly.

"Ms. Toney, I don't *want* to go back to Elise," I said firmly. "Though FYI, they would welcome me with open arms. I chose to apply here at G&L because not only is the company a marketing giant, but it is also the largest minority-owned corporation in America."

"So your plan is to play the race card?" Elena said, shaking her head. "Miss Turner, if you haven't noticed, G&L prides itself on diversity. So you're a sister. So what? That doesn't mean you're qualified, and it surely doesn't mean you're going to get this job."

In less than sixty seconds, she had completely twisted my words around. I decided Elena was a straight-up bitch. "I'm not relying on the fact that I'm a sistah," I said with attitude, professionalism out the door at this point.

"So maybe it's your looks you plan to use," she said, looking from my head down to my open-toed pumps. "I've seen your kind time and time again. The skirts that always seem to ease up during meetings and those low-cut shirts that accidentally fall open like some Janet Jackson wardrobe malfunction." Crossing her arms across her saggy breasts, she sucked on her teeth. "We don't need nor will we allow that here at G&L."

I had chosen to wear my two-piece Calvin Klein suit because it hugged my body in all the right places, and the above-the-knee skirt accentuated my runway model legs. I looked good and like every other normal woman in the world, I felt good when I looked good. It was never my intent to use my body, my face, or my skin tone to land that internship with G&L. However, the ugly face of disapproval Elena was giving me told me she had taken my appearance out of context. "Ms. Toney, I don't have to use my body or my face to get ahead," I said. "Those are just added bonuses I was blessed with."

Her thick, unkempt eyebrows shot up in an arch.

"I am intelligent, educated, and I can do this job better than any of those tight-ass applicants waiting to speak with you. If you're not gonna give me a real chance to prove myself just because of my looks, then I suggest that you step your own appearance and your game up." I crossed my legs, causing my skirt to inch up my thighs. "It's obvious to me that my credentials are not the problem, but my sex appeal is." *"Don't let your smart mouth screw up a good opportunity!"* My mother's words suddenly echoed in my head, but it was too late. I knew before I closed my mouth that I had fucked up with Elena. I watched as she took the application package with my name on it and tossed it to the corner of her desk like yesterday's garbage.

"Miss Turner, we wish you the best in your endeavors, however, your time here is up," she said coldly.

I sat still for a moment, debating as to whether or not to try and redeem myself.

"Goodbye!" she snapped, staring at me.

I decided attempting to kiss the woman's fat ass was not an option. I was halfway out the door, when she called my name.

"Oh and Asia…" she said dryly.

"Yes?" I asked calmly.

"Don't bother with applying here again," she said firmly.

I slammed the door closed behind me. *Hating-ass bitch!* I thought to myself as I walked through the crowded hallway to the elevator.

As I stood waiting for the elevator, a tall, distinguished gentleman walked up and stood beside me. He was slightly older than me, with skin the color of lightly toasted almonds and low-cut hair that was embedded with waves. He was attractive, but at that moment I gave two shits about his looks; I was still fuming about my run-in with Elena.

"Hi. How you doin'?" he spoke as we both watched the numbers on the top of the elevator light up.

"Not good!" I said with attitude.

"What's the problem?" he asked as the elevator doors dinged open.

"Nothing you can do anything about," I snapped, remembering all the extra preparation and time I put in just to work for G&L.

"Oh, I don't know, Miss…"

"Turner," I said flatly

"Miss Turner," he continued, "I'm somewhat of a problem-solver here at G&L. Excuse me for being rude," he said, extending his hand to me. "My name is Parker Bryant."

The mention of his name caught me totally off guard. I had done enough research on G&L to know that Parker Bryant was the CEO. The elevator was almost to the first floor, and I knew I had to act fast if I wanted to get my foot in the door. "Mr. Bryant, please forgive my not-so-pleasant attitude. I was just denied a chance to be a part of this prestigious firm because of my looks," I spat, discreetly telling on Elena.

"You were denied a chance to work for us because of your looks?" he repeated with a puzzled look on his face.

Seeing that I had his attention, I laid it on thick. "Yes. None of my credentials or references were even considered. I have worked hard for this position. I so much wanted to be a part of G &L," I said softly as my eyes watered.

"There has to be an explanation," he said. "I assure you we have a strict policy on discrimination. It's not tolerated here in any way, shape, or form."

"That may be your policy, Mr. Bryant," I sniffled, "but it was not Ms. Toney's."

"Elena Toney?" He frowned.

"Yes. She interviewed me," I whispered sadly. Damn right I snitched on her ass! "I am so devastated right now," I said, squeezing a tear from my eye as the elevator doors opened.

"Miss Turner, I have to go. I apologize, but I'm already late for a very important meeting," he said, reaching inside his jacket pocket. "However, I want you to give me a call tomorrow so we can fix this problem." He handed me his business card and hurried out the building front doors into a waiting black and silver Maybach.

Chapter 2

"Girl, I 'bout reached across the desk and slapped the hell out of that ho!" I said as I rolled my eyes while I told my best friend, Tracy Jenkins, about my interview from hell. I paused as she navigated her brand new BMW Z-8 out into the heavy rush hour traffic. I didn't want to disrupt her concentration, but no sooner had she made the hairpin turn at one of the busiest intersections in the city than I resumed my story.

Tracy and I had been best friends since our freshman year at Howard. We had both spent extensive hours studying and researching the marketing industry, but after the first year of relentless schooling, Tracy had quit and taken up real estate. That move had changed her life dramatically because within a few years, she had managed to secure the two biggest licenses of her life. One was her real estate license, and the other was a marriage license. As luck would have it, Tracy ended up hooking Harold Jenkins, one of the biggest real estate brokers in the city. Following a very brief engagement and subsequent marriage, Tracy happily discovered that she didn't have to sell one single house for her big payday; her husband supplied her every need.

"Oh no she didn't!" Tracey laughed as she pulled her Chanel shades over her eyes. "You're telling me that bitch tried to get grand on my girl, the diva?" Tracy smiled.

"Hell yeah she did!" I exclaimed. "Hating on me because her ass is jacked up."

"She didn't get the memo, A," Tracey said, sucking on her teeth. "We were born beautiful. I know it ain't, fair but it's real. The world will be a much better place as soon as these broads learn and memorize that shit."

It wasn't that my best friend was cocky; she was just confident, and with good reason. At five-six, Tracey had a brown complexion and slanted dark brown eyes. Both of her parents were Black, but considering her eyes, thin lips, and narrow nose, Tracey looked like she could have been of Japanese descent. Much like myself, she had run into her share of haters based solely upon her good looks.

After twenty more minutes of discussing my ordeal at G&L, I changed the subject just as we were pulling up into my apartment complex.

As always, Tracy groaned wearily "Girl, you need to hurry up and get up out of this bullshit. Your ass way too classy to be living like this," Tracy grunted as she weaved her way around several gigantic potholes in the street. "Tearin' my damn car up."

Slightly embarrassed, I casually made light of my situation. "I'll be out of here in due time."

"You're way past due, if you ask me." Tracy studied me like I was a question on a college prep exam. "I don't like to see you living like this. There is a great big world out there, and here you are stuck up in this hellhole like some—"

"Crack-head ho?"

"You said it," Tracy reminded me. "I didn't."

"Girl, I got to get that job at G&L. That's my damn ticket up outta here."

"Well, the sooner you cash in on that ticket the better," Tracey said, shaking her head. "Hell, if Harold didn't have his house rules, you could come stay with us until you get on your feet."

Tracey had told me about Harold's house rules before. He had a strict policy that the only people allowed to sleep under his roof were his kids and the woman he was fucking. This meant he and Tracey would forever have their home to themselves, one because Tracey refused to get pregnant, and two because she was not the type to share her man or his bed.

"It's all good," I said sincerely. "Shit, you got to keep your man happy. Hell, if you don't—"

"The next bitch will," Tracey said, finishing my sentence.

"You know it." I nodded my head in agreement. "You wanna come in for a sec?" I asked politely, secretly hoping she would refuse. I was stressed about my situation and wasn't feeling like girl talk at the moment, but at the same time, I was always willing to make time for my best friend.

"Girl, I would come in, but I got to meet Harold out at the mall for lunch. Call me tonight."

"Okay. I will, and thanks for the ride," I said, relieved that she had declined.

I had almost made it to my front door when I saw Quick Rick approaching me. Rick was a tall, slim brother who closely resembled Chris Rock. He was also the neighborhood dope thief and booster extraordinaire. "What's up, sexy?" Quick Rick asked, stopping beside me.

I continued to approach my door, ignoring him. I had seen Rick several times around my apartment complex, and from what my neighbors told me, Quick Rick could steal the stank out of shit and the diaper off a baby quicker than you could blink. They didn't call him Quick Rick for nothing! Granted, I'm sure their description of him was a bit exaggerated, and I didn't have anything on me of value for him to take, but I wasn't about to take any chances.

"Damn. You can't speak to a brotha?" he asked from behind me. "Stuck-up ass!"

Ignoring him, I slid my key in the lock. Opening the door to the small apartment made my stomach turn. Although I kept my place clean, the one thing I couldn't do anything about was that a roach or two would always greet me just as soon as I stepped into the living room. This time was no exception. I quickly dashed to the kitchen to retrieve one of many cans of Raid I kept under the cabinet. It was then that I noticed the faucet was leaking. "Son of a bitch!" I wailed to myself. If it wasn't roaches and rodents, it was leaky-ass faucets. The building was a shit-hole, and the pot-bellied, toupee-wearing Danny Devito lookalike that passed himself off as my landlord was nothing more than a slumlord. In a fit of anger, I threw a plastic bowl underneath the cabinet to catch the dripping water. Then I made my way back into the living room to battle the roaches.

After taking care of my unwanted guests, I did feel a wee bit better but still decided I needed a more effective stress reliever. I tried to delude myself into believing that getting high was the right solution, but the major problem with that was that it had taken every dime I had to buy the suit for that damn useless interview. And on top of that, I wasn't due to receive any more money from my family for another seven days.

Running out of options just that quickly, I decided to break down and call Steve, a shady brother I had met when I first moved to Georgia. Although Steve wasn't my type, he was cute, with dark skin, a baby face, and a slim physique. He also didn't mind spending his money, which made him a suitable ghetto version of my knight in shining armor whenever I was either stressed out, distressed, or broke.

I held my breath as I dialed his number. The last time the two of us had kicked it, Steve had taken me out to eat and then to the movies. It was cool getting out, but the night did not end well. I loved the fact that Steve had no problem spending his money on me. It was what always came next that pissed my ass off. It didn't matter if the brother had only paid for a burger and a milkshake, he always felt he was automatically entitled to a shot of pussy, but I wasn't feeling Steve that way. I knew he dug me and wanted to fuck me, but I wouldn't think of putting my precious pussy under the care of a muthafucka who wouldn't know how to treat it. Sadly enough, though, I was just about to run out of those patented female lies women invent to keep a man off the booty. I wanted to avoid making Steve mad since I didn't know when I would need him again, so I had to get my shit organized. I decided that if he came to my rescue this time, I would repeat one of my favorite fake-out games, but then I recalled that I had used the lie about being on my period the night we had gone to the movies. As I reflected upon my performance and decided it was an Oscar-worthy performance.

"Oh," I had said, grabbing my stomach dramatically.

"What's wrong, Ma?" Steve had looked genuinely concerned as we pulled out of the parking lot of the theater.

"Damn cramps," I had groaned. "I think my period just came down."

Steve had looked like he either wanted to curse my ass out or to slit my throat. "How you know?" he had asked. "You ain't even checked."

"I'm a woman. I just know."

"Bullshit!" Steve had angrily growled. "I bet it's just something you ate. I'm gonna stop and get you something to coat your stomach."

What the hell!? I had thought to myself. *No, the hell he didn't!* Granted, I had promised him I would finally let him hit it, but he was trippin'! *I know it's written somewhere in the Brothers' Handbook that when a female says she's bleeding, you should dip!* "No, I can feel it," I had told him. I saw I was going to have to go deep, so I had reached way down into my bag of tricks. "I think I just need to go home and lie down for a minute. Can you swing by Walgreens and pick me up some tampons?"

The look on Steve's face had been priceless. Unable to grasp the logistics of my game, he quietly surrendered, mumbled something under his breath about "bullshit", stopped by the drugstore, and then drove me home. I barely had the door closed before Steve drove off, burning rubber, leaving me standing in the parking lot with my purse and tampons in hand. That was three weeks ago, and now I hoped Steve was a forgiving person.

"Hello."

"Hey," I said cheerfully.

"Who dis'?"

"Stop playing, sweetie. You know who this is. It's me, Asia."

"Oh. What up?"

"Shit, tryin' to see if you have some green."

"I thought you quit," he said, sounding like a street-corner philosopher.

"I did, but some things didn't work out," I said honestly. "I need to relieve some stress."

"Oh yeah?" Steve's voice went up an octave. He was

interested, and in his mind had probably already reached the conclusion that today just might be his lucky day. He instantly went into silent mode, and I knew that put the ball right back into my court.

I did as he expected. I broke the silence. "So, you got it or not?

"I ain't got none, but I can get it." Steve sounded sure, but I could tell he wasn't in the mood to get played. He quizzed me openly. "What you got on it?"

So there it is. As always, I would be forced to confess that I was broke. I smacked my lips loudly. "I was hoping you'd have me on it," I spoke sweetly. "My money lookn' a lil' funny right now."

I hated feeling like I was depending on a man, especially one who was always only a couple dollars away from being broke his damn self. But we all know desperate times called for desperate measures.

"You gon' owe for this," Steve barked. "Right?"

I took a second to think about it. "Alright," I said, exhaling, "but it better be some fire."

"I ain't never had no complaints," Steve laughed.

"I was talkin' 'bout the trees," I said, rolling my eyes. "What you talking 'bout?"

"Never mind," Steve chuckled happily. "I got your trifling ass. I'll be through in a minute."

"Don't get lost," I muttered before hanging up the phone.

Thirty minutes later, just as the two women on *The Jerry Springer Show* started to throw chairs at each other, Steve was knocking at my door. "Coming!" I shouted through the door, one hand on the remote and the other reaching for the doorknob. In my mind, I was praying the boy had some good green.

When I flung open the door, he stood there smiling from ear to ear with a bottle of Remy and a box of chicken.

"Damn! I appreciate the special treatment, but I already ate." I stepped to the side. "Come on in."

Entering my apartment, Steve made it a point to brush up against me. Strangely enough, he was bolder than ever before, and even more strange was the look of lust in his eyes, the look on his face that let me know he thought he was gonna get a piece. Granted, I was horny my damn self, but I had no intentions of fulfilling Steve's fantasy. My mind was made up that giving up the pussy was a no-go.

"What's up, baby girl? You looking beautiful as ever," Steve declared, smiling at me. "Here, roll this shit up," he said as he handed me a small plastic bag filled with weed. "Shit so strong you can smell it through the bag," he said proudly. "Muthafucka I got it from say it'll set your ass on fire."

"Thanks for the warning," I said, staring at the dime bag Steve gave me, "but I'm a big girl."

I stared Steve directly in his eyes. "I can handle mine."

"Shit, we'll see," Steve said, laughing lightly. "We will see."

*****

Twenty minutes later, I sat spread-eagled on my couch with Steve licking my clit like an ice cream cone. Some time ago, in what seemed like a fairytale, I vaguely recalled promising myself that I wasn't ever going to give up the pussy, but my high had my coochie throbbing and to not give it up would have seemed like a cruel joke on both of us—not just on Steve, but also on me. I am a hundred percent convinced that I wanted to fuck worse than he did. He was merely in the right place at the right time.

"Mmm," I moaned, pushing his head further down between my legs.

If eating pussy were a career, Steve would have been banking six figures. He slid his tongue in and out of my hot box while massaging my clit between his thumb and index finger.

"Shit!" I screamed, followed by me cumming and squirting. I was still shaking from my original orgasm when I felt Steve slide inside me. *What the fuck?!* I thought.

It was a good thing for Steve that he had a fire mouthpiece, because he wasn't sparking any flames with that dick of his. If it weren't for his sweating and heavy breathing, I wouldn't have even known we were fucking. As fast as he entered me, I heard him groan, "Oh…oh...shit…here it comes," and he exhaled loudly, falling back against the couch.

I glared at his limp, naked dick in disgust, shaking my

head in pity. I wouldn't wish that type of sorry sex on any woman, not even that saggy-tit bitch Elena Toney.

"Put in work, didn't I?"

"Are you fucking serious?!" I snapped, jumping to my feet.

"What?" Steve looked completely clueless as he pulled his pants back up.

"You ain't do shit. Plus, you just nutted in me!" In a flash, I had completely forgotten the fact that Steve was a millisecond man and was now trippin' off the fact that he had put sperm in me without my damn permission.

"So? You actin' like I got something or something," Steve said, staring at me. "Shit, I'm clean."

I slipped my shorts back on and then stood with my hands on my hips. "This ain't just about catching something," I snapped. "What if I get knocked up?" I asked. "Have you forgotten about how lil' babies are made?"

"I thought you was on the pill," Steve responded slowly. The expression on his face was beyond stupid.

"Why would you think that?" I asked, crossing my arms across my chest. "Did I tell you that?"

"I jus' assumed—"

"You know what they say about assuming," I snapped, cutting him off.

If it was possible, his blank expression looked even more stupid.

"It makes an ass out of you," I spat. I rolled my eyes and shook my head. "You're a fucking dumbass."

Abruptly, his expression changed. His eyes, which were already low from his high, became smaller with his anger. "Who the fuck you think you talking to?" He stood, extending his body to his full height.

"I'm talking to your non-fucking ass," I said sarcastically. "As if it's not bad enough, you run up in me raw, last all of ten seconds, then you got the damn nerve to cum in me."

"Fuck you!" he snapped.

"Umm, I think that's what you just *tried* to do," I grumbled, walking to the front door. "Now get the fuck out my house," I said, holding the door open.

"Lose my number, bitch," he spat, pushing past me.

"It's already forgotten," I replied, sucking on my teeth. "Just like your preemie dick!"

I angrily slammed my door shut and locked it. Once I was back inside the privacy of my cheap-ass living room, I yanked all my clothes off, went to the bathroom, and took a long, hot shower, attempting to wash away the memories of Steve and his baby penis.

Chapter 3

The next morning, dark clouds crowded the sky while watering everything below with a heavy downpour of rain. It was a Thursday, and I started out the morning by uttering a string of curse words; I hate rain. Outside my bedroom window, I could hear the splashes of water pinging off the pane so hard it sounded like someone was knocking on the glass. I didn't give a damn that the city was in a drought or that the rain was much needed. All I knew was that I didn't need anything setting my day off on the wrong note, but evidently my plans were no match for whatever plans God had in store. Still, I prayed that as a tiny courtesy, He would turn down the volume on the thunder. That shit scares the hell out of me.

Rolling over in my bed, I tried to figure some things out but ended up with the notion that this was perhaps God's way of telling me to shape up or ship out. I wasn't exactly sure just what that phrase meant, but it had me thinking. Before then, I'd been under the impression that I wasn't truly worthy of divine attention, but maybe I was wrong. I thought maybe it was time for me to either shit or get off the pot. *Life is a battlefield, and if a bitch like me is gonna come up, then I had better get up, get out, and get something*, I told myself.

Ignoring the rain, I hopped out of bed just like Steve, with his little dick, jumped in then out of my coochie. Yes, I was still bitter and cursing his dumbass, but I tried to put it out of my mind. I sprinted to the dresser and popped opened my purse like it was a magic lamp. I fumbled around for a brief second until I located the one item I thought would pave my way to paradise—the sleek, engraved business card Parker Bryant had given me in the elevator at G&L. *Today, Ima get at that ass.*

As usual, when I made up my mind to embark on a mission, I gave myself a pep talk and promised myself it was do-or-die time. According to everything that meant anything, I was already dead financially. One look through my purse would support that concept. Something else I knew was that if I stared into any mirror anywhere in the whole, wide world, the woman who would stare back would be one of the poorest women on the planet. Damn, I was wrecked!

No longer able to disguise my irritation with my empty bank account, I dashed to the window, opened it, and screamed out at the top of my lungs, "I'm sick and tired of being sick and tired!"

"Who gives a damn?!" I heard someone yell back. It was obvious my neighbors were not feeling my affirmation.

"I have got to get out of this dump," I mumbled to

myself. I slammed the window down and decided to make myself useful by coming up with a master plan to get my money up.

Staring at Parker's business card, I played several different scenarios in my head. One of them included me using my womanly assets to get next to the CEO. Laughing loudly, I shook my head at the thought. I was trippin'. I could do the job, and that was enough. I didn't have to use seduction or exploit myself sexually to get ahead. *Besides, that shit only happens in the movies, right? Or does it? Tracey got her big break by putting the pussy on the boss. Why can't I get my foot in the door by using a little female persuasion?* At that moment, I had come into my own little discovery. What I had just discovered was that even if I did look in the mirror and see one of the poorest bitches in the world staring back at me, I would also be looking at one of the finest bitches in the world. And, truth be told, a pretty bitch never has to be a broke bitch because beauty has its privileges and its rewards. I knew if I played my cards right, I could have Parker Bryant on my side using my brain alone, but it wouldn't hurt to sprinkle a little of my female charm in the mix.

In my mind, I studied the image I had of Parker and was totally convinced I could win him over. I still had a few hours to go before I gave his ass a courtesy call at his office, so I listened to the rain and turned on some Nicki Minaj. I was dying to hear the song "Moment 4 Life," where Drake kicked that real talk about how "everybody dies, but not everybody lives." That shit was as hard as penitentiary steel. I refused to let life and the finer things that it held pass me by.

At approximately nine fifteen a.m., I hit Parker up. After giving the secretary my name, I listened impatiently to the sappy hold music until the CEO came on the line. "Miss Turner," he said, sounding pleasantly pleased that I had called. "I've been waiting for your call. We need to talk," he said firmly.

Perfect, I thought. I held my breathing in check, waiting for him to tell me that Elena had filled him in on our interview.

"I'd like to sit down with you and discuss what happened yesterday," he said. "Are you able to come in today?"

I could hardly believe my ears. I was actually receiving a second chance at G &L! I knew there was a possibility that the man, the CEO, only wanted to hear my side of the story in an attempt to forestall a lawsuit; however, something told me this was exactly the break I had been waiting for. "Today would be great," I gushed. "I'd be happy to come in," I added excitedly.

"Wonderful," Parker Bryant said professionally "How does a quarter till two sound?"

"Sounds like I'll be there."

"Perfect. I'll see you then."

Hanging up, I could not contain my excitement as I strolled to my bedroom closet. But quicker than Steve's pathetic nut, my smile turned upside down, flipping into an ugly-assed frown as I realized I didn't have shit to wear. The only gear in my wardrobe that screamed "sexy corporate executive" was the one I had wasted on my interview with Elena Toney. Everything else I had was cheap or boring or both. Shaking my head, I weighed my options before finally choosing a black jacket and matching slacks. The one-button jacket required a blouse underneath, so that was where I decided to "sex it up" a little bit. I decided to add my leopard print halter, then throw on a pair of four-inch leopard print pumps to complete my ensemble.

Tired of trying to trick myself, I finally admitted that the outfit, though alright, wasn't hitting it. For my one forty-five, I wanted to step out in some shit as fly as a model on a Paris runway. I knew in order to make it happen, I had better get busy.

*****

Saks Fifth Avenue was my store of choice, and spying all the expensive apparel made me feel as happy as a crack-head on buy-one-get-one-free day down on the block.

I was now dressed in the black jacket and matching slacks, so I didn't look like a shoplifter, although that didn't stop me from sweating. My forehead was damp with perspiration, and I jumped when the preppy saleswoman asked me if she could be of any assistance. *Yeah*, I thought to myself, *you can get lost!* However, I smiled while looking into her bright blue eyes then said, "Not at the moment, thank you. I'm just looking."

Just like I thought it would, my mind started playing games with me because everywhere I looked, I thought I saw a plain-clothes police or a mall security guard following me, waiting on me to stick a dress or a pair of slacks into my empty shopping bag, but the prospect of going to jail was not going to stop me from looking good at that meeting with the gorgeous CEO.

When my phone vibrated inside my purse, I didn't dare answer it. *Whoever it was is just gonna have to wait,* I thought. *But what if it's Parker Bryant?* I opened my purse, turned the phone over, and peeked at the number. It was my mother, the last person in the world I wanted to speak to at that moment. *Leave a message*, I thought to myself. I love my mama, but she had perfect timing when it came to picking the wrong time. I assumed she was calling to give me another one of her spur-of-the-moment lectures or to remind that I needed to hurry up and get a job so I could support her. Either way, I didn't want to hear what she had to say.

Feeling spooked by the call, I walked around to the part of the store where the bathrooms were located, pondering on something I had heard about some shit called "Mother Wit". The theory is that the bond between a mother and her children is so powerful that a mama can sense when one of her children is up to no good, that she can feel it in her bones when one of her rugrats is 'bout to do something stupid. Thinking about that, I felt jinxed, but then I remembered that my mother was only my mother through the umbilical cord. Hell, that was cut at birth. My father's mama was the one who nurtured and took care of me as a child. My father, Joseph, died when I was three, and my birth mother, Angela, left me in his mother's care 75 percent of the time. It was my grandmother, Grams, who attended every school event, encouraged me to further my education, and dropped a few extra dollars in my purse from time to time. If it hadn't been for Grams, I probably woulda been standing on someone's block turning tricks. If Grams had been the one calling, I would have hauled ass to get out of the store, but since it was only my mama, I quickly pushed the theory of Mother's Wit out of my mind. My bumming got-an-excuse-for-everything mama couldn't sense her own problems, so I knew she would be clueless to the problems of anybody else, including me.

I pulled back the drapes of one of the dressing rooms and plopped down on one of the wooden benches inside; I needed a "me" moment. I wiped the sweat from my brow and took a deep breath. I was trying to build up the courage to do what I felt had to be done. I pulled myself up from the bench, reminding myself that I had no time to waste. I had work to do.

Walking out of the dressing room, I had never felt more alone in my life, but no one ever told me life was sweet. I told myself that it was a hard-knock life, but it was all I had at the moment, so I had to seize any opportunity that came my way or else I would get left behind.

After less than ten minutes, I was amped, pumped up

with so much false courage that if a security fool had got up in my face, trying to prevent me from stealing the hottest outfit in that joint, I would've slapped the shit out of his rent-a-cop ass.

I headed around to a rack of Dior dresses and eyed a sexy dark blue silk shirred number. The dress was bad as hell hanging on the rack, and I knew it would be a killer on my body. I ran my hand across the delicate material while eyeing the creation more closely.

"Miss, you look like you fixin' to do somethin' real foul."

I spun around on my toes like a ballerina, and just as I was about to spit out a couple of curse words to let the man have it, I relaxed when I recognized him. "Quick Rick," I whispered breathlessly. "You scared the hell out of me."

"What you trembling for?" he asked, sucking his teeth. "You up to no good?"

It was then that I decided taking the dress myself was not an option, but Rick was. "I need a favor," I said sweetly.

"Oh yeah?" Rick said, smiling brightly. "What's that?"

"See this dress?" I asked quietly. "Can you get it for me?"

"Can you say half-price?"

I exhaled lightly. I knew most of the boosters charged half the list price of the garments they stole, but I couldn't even afford to pay that. "I'm broke," I admitted. I lowered my eyes seductively, hoping Rick would start thinking with the head in his pants and give me a free pass.

"Then you best get that muthafucka yo damn self," he said seriously. "But let me get missin' first, 'cause I don't want them White folks to think we together. I been watching your ass for about twenty minutes, and I see you don't know what the fuck you doing."

"Unlike you, theft is not my chosen profession," I snapped.

"And unlike yo stuck-up ass, I don't need that damn dress," he snorted.

"Come on Rick," I said, practically begging, "just do this one thing for me. I'll pay you back as soon as I can."

"You wantin' favors and shit now?" he asked. "Hell, just yesterday, you acted like I didn't exist. Now you askin' for favors and shit? How I know I can trust you to get my paper up if I snatch that dress for you?"

"I promise—"

"Dem famous last words," Quick Rick cracked knowingly.

"I'm good for it," I said solemnly.

"You want that shit bad," he said, rubbing the patch of hair on his chin. "Tell you what. I got a better plan. Let's go to the dressing room where you just came from, and you show me how bad you want this dress."

"What?"

"You deaf now?" he asked, flashing his brown eyes at me. "You want that shit, you gotta get down for it."

"You want me to fuck you in the dressing room?" I asked, disgusted.

"Didn't nobody ask for no pussy," he chuckled. I was relieved until he said, "I want some head."

"You can't be serious."

"Look, you wastin' my damn time, woman," he huffed. "You want that shit or not?"

"When am I gonna get my dress?"

"As soon as I bust a nut, it's on," Quick Rick said, impatiently rubbing his crotch. "Shit, I can't wait to stick this dick down your throat."

The thought of Rick's stick in my mouth made me want to puke, and not because I thought it was big enough to gag me. "Forget it," I said, shaking my head.

"Fuck you then," Quick Rick said as he started to walk away.

I felt defeated as I stared at the silk ensemble hanging on the rack. "Where you going?" I asked, quickly capturing his attention. "The dressing room is over there."

* * * * *

At one thirty sharp, I entered G&L with my head held high and my hips swinging. The Dior dress hugged my body like a well-oiled glove. The olive-skinned security guard sitting at the visiting desk gave me a small smile and the once-over with his eyes. I smiled back but dismissed his eye-gawking just as I always did when men stared at me. I was accustomed to men (and even the occasional woman) doing a double-take when they saw me. I can't say I blame them. When I'm on top of my game, I'm too fly for my own damned good.

At five-five, with smooth skin the color of cocoa, dark

brown eyes, high cheekbones, and full lips, I was a dime-piece. And when you add to that physical equation my full, perky breasts, onion ass, and long legs, you have a package that won't quit. Even though I'm a top-of-the-line ten, I still feel underrated.

I smiled at the man once more before jumping on the elevator and pressing the button for the tenth floor. "I'm Asia Turner," I purred with confidence and authority. "I'm here to see Mr. Bryant."

"Have a seat, Miss. Turner," the receptionist replied. "Mr. Bryant is running a little late from an earlier meeting, but he will be with you shortly."

I nodded and then eased down into one of the smooth leather chairs. I was in my own zone, thinking about the task I before me, when I was snatched back to reality by a dreaded voice.

Looking up, I watched Elena as she laughed and conversed with a tall handsome brother wearing a double-breasted suit. "It's such a small world," she squealed. "I've been a member of New Life Baptist ever since I moved to Georgia."

"I knew you looked familiar," the man said. "My father is Elder Fredrick Harston, the new associate minister, and I've been the drummer there for the last two months. You should consider joining the mass choir." He gazed at Elena fondly. "Let me guess…you're a soprano, right?"

"Second soprano and first alto," Elena chuckled.

I couldn't believe my eyes; the bitch was actually

blushing!

"I was close," the man flirted. "Rehearsal is Saturday at noon, and I would love to see you there."

I laughed to myself. Elena looked old enough to be his mother, not to mention that she was a hot mess, and that was putting it kindly. She was definitely one female who could use a full body makeover. *What is he thinking?* I wondered.

"Well, this has been a wonderful interview," Elena commented, shaking the man's hand, "and I'm sure Mr. Bryant will be quite impressed with your resume."

"The pleasure has been all mine." The visitor smiled seductively. "Thank you, and I do hope to see you Saturday."

I was hoping she would go the opposite direction and I could avoid an uncomfortable confrontation, but as luck would have it, she looked up, and our eyes instantly locked. The schoolgirl smile she was wearing just seconds earlier immediately dissolved, and I swear I could see steam billowing out her ears as she marched in my direction. "What are you doing here?" she asked, stopping in front of me.

"How are you this afternoon, Ms. Toney?" I faked a smile. "It's so good to see you again."

"You can drop the little act, Miss Turner." Elena eyes narrowed, and she stood wide-legged with her hands on her hips. "I don't care if you beg, I am not giving you another chance."

"When did you give me the first one?" I snapped evilly. I wanted to remind her that her fat ass was so busy hating on my phat ass that she didn't even give me the opportunity to prove myself. However, I decided to stay in character and to continue playing my innocent role. "Ms. Toney, I apologize that the two of us got off on the wrong foot," I said somberly while staring up at her. "I'd really like for us to start over."

Shaking her head, Elena laughed. "That phony schoolgirl innocence may work for the men you manipulate," she said, "but I'm not a sucker for a pretty face."

"I can't help how I look. Why can't you get over that? It's not fair that you judge me on what you see on the outside," I said as my voice trembled. Being somewhat of a drama queen, I can cry on demand—another one of my specialties—so when I batted my long, luscious eyelashes, they were streaked with tears.

Shaking her head, Elena laughed.

"Would someone like to tell me what's going on here?"

At the sound of Parker Bryant's voice, the laughter dissipated.

"Mr. Bryant?" Elena said, adjusting her jacket. "What are you doing down here?"

The CEO stared at the woman and then, with a gentlemanly flair, reached into his jacket pocket and handed me a silk handkerchief.

Sniffing loudly, I sobbed a muffled "Thank you," before taking the cloth from his hand.

Elena looked like she wanted to choke my ass and probably would have tried it, but Parker Bryant was not finished with either of us just yet.

"I asked a question," he said firmly, "and I want an answer. Now what is going on here?" he repeated.

"Nothing, Mr. Bryant. Nothing at all." Elena's voice cracked as she spoke. "Miss Turner dropped by to see me, but I explained to her that I've already selected my candidate for the internship, and she was just leaving."

"Actually, Miss Turner is here to see me."

The look on Elena's face was priceless! She was completely caught off guard. "For…for what?" she asked, looking from her boss to me.

"I don't think that's any of your concern." Parker Bryant's tone was pleasant, but there were enough undercurrents to let Elena know she was overstepping her bounds.

"I'm sorry," she said. The arrogance she had displayed just a few minutes earlier was completely gone. She was now as silent and docile as a child being reprimanded by her father.

"You don't owe *me* any apology," the CEO said sternly, "but you should get back to work." Turning his full attention to me, he smiled warmly. "This way, Miss Turner."

With polished elegance, I slowly rose to follow my Prince Charming down a long corridor. Just before I entered the sparkling, clean corner office with the magnificent view, I nonchalantly gazed over my shoulder; sure enough, Elena watched me with a look of stunned amazement on her face. I winked at her, and she stalked off, but I knew it wasn't over between us.

* * * * *

"I must say I'm impressed," Parker Bryant said, staring intently at my resume. "With recommendations like these, along with your impressive track record, you can pretty much make the corporate world stand still and wait for you." The CEO chuckled. "I have to admit it has been quite a while since I have seen such impeccable credentials."

After I'd concluded my crying spell and shared all the ugly details of my interview with Elena with him, we both relaxed. From there, the two of us engaged in an intense but pleasant question-and-answer session. Parker was easy to talk to and even easier on the eyes. The man was fine, to put it lightly.

"I think with your talents and the proper mentoring, you could be a great addition to the G&L team. However, it does concern me that you have already had an unpleasant encounter with another valued member of the G&L family. We are a team here, and though our job descriptions may be different, we all act as a single unit. I look unfavorably on dissension in the ranks. It is not good for company morale, which I'm quite sure you understand."

In the flash of a heartbeat, I could sense my chances of working at G&L about to evaporate quicker than a snowball in hell. It suddenly appeared that Elena would get the last laugh which would, no doubt, make her have an orgasm. I didn't feel it was fair, but sometimes the Plain Jane bitch wins out over the beauty queen. That's just the way it is.

"Here at G&L," Parker Bryant continued, "we believe in working through our differences."

I looked up at him with raised eyebrows, hoping I had heard him right. I watched his lips move so I wouldn't miss what came out of his mouth next.

"That said, welcome to G&L, Asia."

I felt like my heart would leap out of my chest. "Are you…are you serious?" I stammered, practically bouncing up and down in my chair.

"I'm always serious," he smiled.

"Thank you!" I screamed, jumping to my feet. To say that I was overwhelmed would be an understatement. Thoughts of how I planned to spend my first paychecks danced in my head. *Car? Check. Move out of the ghetto? Check. Nice clothes without having to blow that thieving asshole in the dressing room? Check.*

"Miss Turner?"

The sound of my name snapped me back to reality. "I'm sorry," I smiled, sitting back down.

"Understandable," he laughed lightly. "Now, keep in mind that this offer is contingent upon you passing a criminal background check and drug screening."

Oh shit! Flashbacks of my smoke session danced through my mind like a bad movie, but I had to play it to the end. "No problem," I lied. "I'm clear in both departments."

"Wonderful," he said, leaning back in the leather high-back chair. "I'll have my assistant Jessica get together your new hire paperwork and schedule a time for you to go to the lab for the drug test." He stood, then extended his hand to me. "Welcome aboard, Miss Turner."

Chapter 4

"Girl, you are a lifesaver," I said, smiling at Tracey. After leaving my interview, I told Tracey about my night with Steve, and she drove me by the Cigar Shop to pick up a bottle of Q-Carbo and a Q Clean tablet.

"I know, I know," she said, rolling her eyes. "Does that shit really work?" she asked, reading the label on the back of the bottle.

"The hell if I know," I said, "but desperate times call for desperate measures."

"Down a gallon of water and send up a prayer, and I'm sure you'll be fine," Tracey said. "And what the hell you doing fucking with Steve?" she asked, placing her hand on her hip.

"It was a spur-of-the-moment decision," I said, shrugging my shoulders. "A bad one at that. But he did have that fiyah," I laughed, reminiscing.

"Steve got that good dick?" Tracey asked with a grin.

"Hell no!" I said quickly. "I was talking 'bout the green."

"Oh. Well, how was the dick?" Tracey asked curiously.

"A waste of my time," I declared, "but he is on point

with his tongue."

"Good tongue, bad dick?" Tracey asked.

"Smoking tongue, teenie dick," I informed her.

"Teenie?"

"Like a damn newborn."

"Why the hell he even pull that thing out?" Tracey said frowning. "He knew what he was working with before he dropped his damn draw's. They kill me with that shit." She laughed lightly. "They could at least give a chick some warning."

"I think they should have to walk around with a sign attached to their shirt," I joked. "Warning! Lil' dick here. The contents of this package are likely to disappoint. Fuck at your own risk!"

We both cracked up at the same time.

"But the mouthpiece was on point?" she asked again.

"Yes, ma'am!"

"Good tongue, bad dick," Tracey recited. "Hmm. Either way you go, it's a bad combination." She laughed. "You can't have one without the other. No woman wants just good meat all the time," she continued. "You got to be able to clean the plate. And no woman wants a man with good eating habits only. You gots to be able to beat the coochie up."

"True," I laughed, exhaling deeply.

"Well, If all else fails with your drug test, you can come work for me," she said. "I need a secretary."

"I'd never be satisfied being no secretary," I told her. "I want the big dollars and the corner office."

"I feel ya, A."

"Besides, why do you need a secretary?" I asked, frowning, "You don't do any work."

"Excuse me, hater?" she said, sucking on her teeth. "I work very hard."

"Trace, you are the only realtor I know who hasn't sold a single home, yet you still get a commission check."

"Hey, I still put in my share of work," she laughed, tossing her sandy mane over her shoulders. "Backing all this ass up is a full-time job." She stood up and turned, giving me full view of her ample backside.

"Get that thing out of my face." I frowned, looking away. Tracey gave the term "ass for days" a whole new meaning. She had what I like to call a "global ass," an ass big enough to cover the whole world. Granted, I was exaggerating somewhat, but her butt was ridiculously big. For the most part, Tracey would be considered petite. She had small A-cup breast and a tiny waist, but what she lacked in her upper body, she made up for in the rear.

"I'm just saying A," she laughed, dropping back down on the couch, "that Harold is a beast, and he loves—and I do mean *loves—when* I'm face down, and as—"

"I get it, I get it," I said, cutting her off.

"I'm telling you," she said, smiling, "it's a full-time job keeping my man happy."

"And you get compensated very well," I teased.

"As I should!"

"Well, I plan to get my big paycheck soon," I said

seriously. "Success is my only option."

"You will, A," she said with a smile. "What's for you is yours, and no one can keep it from you. But you got to stop having those spur-of-the-moment smoke breaks," Tracey said, shaking her head. "And stop dealing with brothers who can't afford and don't deserve you."

"You're preaching to the choir," I mumbled. "Steve was a one-time thing, and that was only because I was super horny and needed to get laid."

"I feel you, even if you didn't feel him," she teased. "Well, I gotta go," Tracey said, sliding her Gucci bag onto her shoulder as she stood. "Harold and I have a dinner date."

"Must be nice to have a man to wine and dine you," I said, exhaling dramatically.

"Last time I checked, you were single by choice," she said, rolling her eyes. "We both know you don't want to keep a man."

"You're right," I agreed. "I want *men*."

Tracey looked at me with her eyebrows raised. "Slut," she purred, giving me a sly grin.

"No," I said quickly. "I want *dead* men—dead presidents, to be exact."

Tracey looked completely clueless.

"I want money," I said firmly.

"I'm all for the finer things in life," Tracey said, opening my front door, "but remember money does not make the world go 'round."

"You're right," I agreed, "but it damn well does fund the tickets for the flight and the trip around it!"

Chapter 5

Adjusting my button-front silk blouse and pencil skirt, I sat quietly listening to my trainer go over our morning briefings. Although my outfit was business cute and sexy, it was a dramatic plunge from the Dior dress I rocked when Parker interviewed me. After slumming to my lowest to get Quick Rick to boost the dress for me, I decided to use other means to fatten my wardrobe; I opted to pawn the few things I still owned of value and then hopped on the shuttle bus to TJ Maxx. One of the items I pawned was the one-carat sapphire-diamond ring my grandmother had given me for my college graduation. I swore to myself that I would return and get my ring as soon as I could. All the other items could be replaced, but the ring was irreplaceable and had been in my family for years. My grandmother had chosen to give it to me because she felt I would forever cherish it. I felt like I had disappointed her in more ways than one, and pawning the ring was no exception, but my desire to dress to impress was irresistible.

After successfully passing my drug screen, I was officially on the G&L payroll, one step closer to financial freedom. Once I had my drug test out the way, I was able to start my internship the following Monday, and that was just the beginning. I still had to land a permanent position with G&L, which meant I needed to cancel the other interns selected for the program ASAP. At the end of our six-week internship, one candidate would be selected for a position working in the Advertising Department, and I planned to be that intern. My goal was to bypass all the petty bullshit and go straight to the top using everything I had in my arsenal.

My first day was filled with a tour of G&L's beautiful offices, which included an indoor gym, daycare, and fully staffed cafeteria. I also spent my first day getting to know my training supervisor, Nathaniel McLain, a short brother with dark skin and a medium build.

I also met the other two interns who had been selected for the program. One was a tall, thin, blonde named Bethany. She had a pretty face and bright blue eyes the color of the ocean. She was wafer thin but pretty nonetheless. When I first saw her, I knew she looked familiar, but it wasn't until she advised me that she had been the one that had wished me luck the day I interviewed with Elena that I remembered who she was. I'll admit I felt a surge of guilt about how I had dismissed her well wishes that day in the waiting room. The truth was, I needed luck and then some to get hired at G&L.

The second intern, Jamel, was tall with caramel-colored skin, handsome, and dressed like he stepped right out the pages of a men's fashion magazine. He was also the man I had witnessed flirting with Elena on the day Parker hired me. I wondered exactly how far he had gone with the woman to secure his spot in the program. The thought of her all over him turned my stomach.

G&L normally only allowed two interns, but due to Parker pulling rank and hiring me, I was the third wheel. I didn't let this shake me. I was confident that I would prove myself worthy of the position in no time. In addition to my confidence, I had what I felt was the upper hand. I had, after all, already captured the attention of the CEO.

Parker further confirmed this when he entered the training room that day. "Good morning," he said, standing in the doorway.

"Good morning," Bethany said enthusiastically. Bethany was always the first one to say something.

Rolling my eyes at her, I turned to face the door and give the sexy CEO my undivided attention.

"Good morning, Mr. Bryant," I heard Nathaniel and Jamel say one after the other.

Standing tall wearing a dark Armani suit and soft pink dress shirt with a silk platinum-colored tie, Parker looked at me. "It's good to see you again, Asia."

"Thank you," I smiled. "It's good to see you." There was brief second of no verbal communication between the two of us. At the time, I didn't know what Parker's eyes were saying to me, but I was using mine to tell him I was the one he needed to add to his team permanently.

Clearing his throat, Nathaniel interrupted my silent communication. "Class, Mr. Bryant is the CEO here at G&L. Mr. Bryant, this is Bethany Hall and Jamel Harston." Nathaniel continued, "and I see you've already met Asia."

"Hello, Bethany," Parker said, pulling his eyes from mine. "Hello, Jamel." Parker nodded in each of their directions, then turned to Nathaniel. "I'll get out of your way," he said. "I look to see more from this group, and I expect great things. Have a good day, all," Parker said pleasantly. He turned to leave, but before doing so he flashed his eyes in my direction one last time.

In a way, the beginning of my employment at G&L was like the beginning of a new romance. Nathaniel provided us breakfast and lunch, and we spent the majority of our eight-hour day watching PowerPoint presentations about the company and its founder. By the third day, I knew my new hire honeymoon was officially over, and it was time to buckle down.

"Today you get your first assignments," Nathaniel said as he walked around the table passing out presentation folders. "The three of you are to come up with an ad pitch for a new fragrance line for one of our clients. Inside you will find all the details of what our client is looking for. Your presentations are due a week from today."

Flipping through the folder, I glanced over the information inside. I was ecstatic that the client was Juicy Couture.

"You will be presenting your pitches to the head of our

Ad Sales and Marketing teams. The person with the best campaign will win a lunch with our CEO."

The mere mention of Parker's name made me sit at attention. I knew I had to be the one to win the contest and the lunch date with Parker.

"Any questions?" Nathaniel asked, looking around the room.

The three of us shook our heads.

"Great," Nathaniel said lightly. "Good luck with your pitches. Now, for today's assignments," he continued, "Asia, you will report to the mailroom."

What the hell? I thought to myself. *The mailroom? He can't be serious.* I waited for Nathaniel to laugh or give me some indication he was joking, but he never did.

Instead, he turned to Bethany and said, "Bethany, you're going to see Ramona in the Ad Sales Department, and Jamel, you're to report to Adam in Marketing."

Ain't that some shit?

"Learn as much as you can," Nathaniel continued, while walking to the door. "I'll see the three of you back here at noon." He strolled out the room before either of us could respond.

"See you at lunch," Bethany said, flashing me a sly smile.

I rolled my eyes as I watched her walk out the door with her head held high.

"Bye, sexy," Jamel said sweetly. He winked his eye at me then exited the room, leaving me sitting alone.

Standing, I exhaled, trying hard not to take my mundane assignment as an act of favoritism, but I couldn't ignore the facts.

In the short time we had spent together in training, I had already concluded that Bethany was a brown-nosing kiss-ass. Bethany was practically sucking Nathaniel's dick for attention, bringing him coffee and being overly eager to answer any question Nathaniel threw out. Nathaniel had yet to show her any special attention or favors and always appeared to be on a professional level, but men can be suckers for a pretty face and ass, no matter how flat that ass may be. It was quite possible he was playing into her quest to be his favorite.

Jamel, on the other hand, didn't go out of his way to play nice with Nathaniel. He was too busy flirting with every pair of tits and nice ass in the building. Jamel was cocky and an obvious womanizer, but he did have Elena on his side, and that was an issue for me. Every day she managed to make a special appearance in the training room to see if there was anything she could do to help us. She spoke aloud in front of the class, but each time, her eyes would subtly land on Jamel, and a goofy I-need-to-get-laid grin would creep across her face. She also made it clear whenever the two of us would pass each other in the halls that I was still on her shit list by cutting her eyes in my direction or exhaling loudly. All these factors had me wonder if they were the reason behind me getting dumped in the mailroom.

*****

Oscar, the mailroom supervisor, was an older Black man who bared a striking resemblance to Bill Cosby. He was laidback and made my time on postal duty a breeze. He'd give me instructions on what he wanted me to do and then do it himself. The arrangement worked perfectly for the both of us. Oscar did all the work while I pretended not to notice him sneaking peeks at my breasts or cleavage.

"You know, some of the best of the best interns served their time down here in the mailroom," he said to me as he sorted through the stack of outgoing mail.

"Really?"

"Yes, ma'am." He laughed, rubbing the thick gray hair on his chin. "I guess that means you're something special."

"I guess," I exhaled.

"You gotta be," Oscar smiled, staring at me. "Only the best get the pleasure of working their way up."

I watched as he took a long sip from his plastic coffee mug.

"Ain't nothing wrong with climbing your way up from the bottom, baby girl," he said, swallowing loudly. "Hell, that's what I did!"

I silently wondered if Oscar realized the mailroom was at the bottom of the corporate totem pole. My expression must have given him indication that I thought he was crazy, because he looked at me and laughed.

"Naw, I ain't crazy, so you can stop looking at me like

I'm stupid," he chuckled, shaking his head. "Hell, the mailroom *was* my upgrade, baby girl."

I frowned, wondering if Oscar had a little more than coffee in his cup.

"Hell, I used to be the janitor!" he blurted, watching me.

I giggled lightly, then nodded my head in agreement. "I guess this is a step up for you then," I said sweetly.

"You better believe it," he said, sucking on his false teeth. "I'll take tossing out mail over wiping up piss any day!"

"Me, too, Oscar."

Oscar spent the next few minutes educating me on some of the major players at G&L, letting me know who was cool and who was strictly business. He also filled me in on the office gossip—all the who, what, when, and where. I absorbed every word of knowledge he provided me and made mental notes. If any of the people he schooled me on got in my way, I planned to use my knowledge to cancel their ass. I was hungry as hell for success, and no one—and I do mean no one—was gonna prevent me from getting it.

"How's it going down here?"

I had been so engulfed in my conversation with Oscar that I hadn't noticed Nathaniel entering the mailroom. Hopping up out of my chair, I smoothed my hands down over the front of my skirt.

"It's going great." I smiled nervously. I was ultra-paranoid that Nathaniel had caught me sitting down doing nothing on the job. I was already feeling like he thought I was the black sheep of the class, and I knew catching me doing nothing would not help my case.

Laughing, Oscar looked from me to Nathaniel. "She's an excellent student, Nate," he said. "One of the best yet."

"Come on now, O," Nathaniel said, staring at me. "You're trying to tell me she's better than me?" he asked, speaking to Oscar with his eyes still locked on me.

"I sure am," Oscar said, "and she's prettier!"

I smiled sweetly at Oscar, then turned back to look at Nathaniel. He nodded his head and then smiled slightly.

"I won't argue with you on that one," he mumbled. There was an unspoken message in his eyes, and a silence lingered between the three of us until Nathaniel finally said, "Well, I'll let the two of you get back to work. See you at noon, Asia," he said, sliding his hands into the front pockets of his pants. "Catch you later, O."

Oscar looked from Nathaniel to me and then back to Nathaniel. "Catch you later, young blood," he said, clearing his throat.

The two of us watched as Nathaniel slowly eased out the room backwards.

"I'll be damned," Oscar laughed lightly. "Young blood is a lil' sweet on you!"

"What?" I frowned, then laughed loudly, trying to play it off. "Oscar, you're trippin'."

"I've been here for ten years," Oscar said, running a stack of envelopes through the postage meter. "I was here when Nate started three years ago. I've seen him work with a lot of trainees, and only a select few have been sent down here to work with me. Not once has Nate come down here to check on a trainee."

"That could mean he doesn't trust my work ethics," I said, still kicking myself that Nathaniel had caught me being unproductive on the job.

"I'm telling you what I can see," Oscar said seriously, "and I see that that man got a thang for you."

*****

For lunch, I decided to enjoy some sunshine by sitting out on the covered patio adjacent to the G&L cafeteria. It was mid-August, and the temperature was in the mid-seventies. There was a light breeze, making the weather comfortable and beautiful. I sat alone on the patio, enjoying a grilled chicken salad while flipping through the latest issue of *Essence* magazine.

"Mind if I join you?"

Looking up, I saw Jamel standing beside the table, holding one of the plastic trays from the cafeteria. He pulled out a chair and sat down before I could respond.

"Guess not," I said. I watched as he set down his tray and removed his jacket.

"So how were things in the mailroom?" he asked, looking over at me.

I couldn't tell if he was genuinely concerned or if he was attempting to be sarcastic. "It went well," I said. "And how did it go with Adam?"

"Okay," he said nonchalantly. "The man's cocky as hell, but other than that, it went well."

"So you were in the company of your own kind?" I said.

Jamel laughed at my comment, obviously unaware that I was dead serious. "I'm not cocky," he said, licking his lips. "I'm convinced. Give me a try, and I'll convince you of a few things."

He was openly flirting with me, but unlike the other women I saw in the office that seemed to melt at the sound of his voice, I was not buying his playboy persona. There was something peculiar about Jamel that I had yet to put my finger on—something that told me he wasn't the smooth pussy-playing church boy he appeared to be. "I'm convinced too," I laughed. "I'm convinced you're full of shi—"

"Mr. Harston and Miss Turner."

I turned around and found Elena standing behind the two of us with her arms crossed. She looked at Jamel and smiled, then looked at me and puckered her lips like she had a bitter taste in her mouth.

"Hello, Ms. Toney." Jamel smiled, showing his perfect set of teeth. "How are you?" he asked.

"I'm well," she said with enough sugar in her voice she could have sweetened a lemon. "How is training going?" she asked.

"Not bad at all," Jamel stated. "I feel truly blessed to

have received this opportunity."

"Well, you are well deserving." Elena smiled.

"You are too kind," Jamel said smoothly, playing Elena like a baby grand piano.

If he wasn't already tapping that ass, he was only a phone call way. I was sure all Elena had to do was see his name on the caller ID, and she'd get naked!

"And how are you adapting, Miss Turner?" Elena cut her eyes in my direction.

"I'm adapting perfectly, *Elena*," I said, putting emphasis on her name. I was intentionally pushing her buttons and enjoying every second of it.

Her eyebrows shot up from behind her wire-rimmed glasses. "You can call me Ms. Toney," she said firmly.

"But Ms. Toney is so impersonal," I said innocently, "considering we're like one big happy family here at G&L. I was just about to tell Jamel that I am going to make it my personal business to attend one of the services at New Life Baptist. I would love to hear you sing," I added. "Second soprano, first alto, right?" If I could have sold Elena at that moment, her ass would have been packaged and shipped to the highest bidder.

"I've yet to join the choir," Elena said, clearing her throat. "However, we welcome all visitors."

"Perfect," I purred. "Jamel remind me to give you my number so you can pick me up."

A small frown crept across Elena's face, like a billboard flashing how jealous she was.

I decided to play with her a little. "In fact, Jamel, the two of us should really get together sometime after work for a little one-on-one Bible study," I added, licking my lips. Grabbing my tray and magazine, I stood up. "We can have a hallelujah good time together!" I said suggestively.

Jamel smiled brightly, but Elena looked liked she wanted to pull every strand of hair from my scalp.

Try it, trick, I thought. I stepped past her swaying my hips like I was moving to the beat of a drum.

* * * * *

I reclined in the passenger seat of Tracey's car as she zoomed past the potholes in the lot of my complex until finally pulling up in front of my building. After listening to her tell me about her day in the world of real estate, I finally told her about the events of mine, including my time in the mailroom.

"So this dude Jamel is screwing the chick from Human Resources?"

"I don't know if he's physically screwing her," I said, turning up my nose. The thought of anyone humping Elena made me want to gag. "But he is definitely screwing with her mind. And to some women, a mind fuck is ten times worse than getting the actual dick," I added.

"True," Tracey agreed, nodding her head. "You need to watch her ass and cover yours."

"Who you tellin'?" I asked. "Please believe I plan to."

"Speaking of covering your own ass," Tracey said,

glancing over at me, "I received a voicemail from an Elena chick wanting to verify employment for you with Elise."

"What?" My pulse immediately accelerated to the point that I could hear my heart pounding in my ears. "When, and what did that bitch say?"

"This afternoon," Tracey said. "She said she's doing a background check and you provided my number as the contact."

"Fuck!" I snapped, shaking my head.

"Calm down, A," Tracey said soothingly, looking over at me. "I called her back and told her you were a wonderful employee and eligible for rehire."

The fact that Tracey had stood behind me and the lie I told was little comfort to me. I knew if Elena was inquiring about my work history and how legit I was, eventually the truth behind my credentials would be exposed. Even though I did graduate from Howard and had a letter of recommendation, the truth was I'd never stepped foot in Elise. So, when Elena suggested there was a reason I might be ineligible for rehire with the company, she was way off the mark. In order for me not to be eligible for rehire, I would have had to have actually worked for the company in the first place. "Thanks, Trace," I said sincerely, "but I'm still shook."

"Why?"

"Because the chick from HR *is* Elena!"

Tracey looked at me with raised eyebrows. "Damn," she mumbled. "She's relentless."

"Hell, she hates me," I said. "I should have expected that shit." Flashbacks of our earlier conversation popped in my mind. Until I was informed Elena was doing her research on me, I had felt I had the upper hand. The ball was now in her court, and it was, without a doubt, time for me to make a steal.

"It will work, A," Tracey said, giving my hand a squeeze. "Either that or we'll make this Elena chick disappear, whichever comes first," she said lightly.

Giving her a faint smile, I pretended to ponder on her words. "Well, I'm not above violence," I said seriously.

Taking my words as an attempt to be funny, Tracey laughed. "That will be our very last resort," she said. "Something tells me you're gonna find another option soon and very soon."

"I hope so."

"Well, I have got to get going," Tracey said, looking at the diamond watch on her wrist. "Harold has been trippin' the last few days, expecting me to cook and shit."

"Um, that's what wives do," I said, forcing a smile, still trying to process the information Tracey had given me about Elena snooping around in my past.

"What the hell ever," she said, smacking her lips. "He knew when he married me that I ain't the domesticated type. In addition to his demands for home-cooked meals, he's chosen to put me on a budget!" She whined.

"The economy is bad, Trace. Everyone should be on a budget."

She looked at me like I was speaking some foreign language. "You need to hurry up and blow up, because living among the peasants has tainted your thoughts, girl."

"Wasn't it you who told me the other day that money doesn't make the world go 'round?" I asked with raised eyebrows.

"Uh, yeah, but that was before my man started trying to cut my spending off and started trying to turn me into damn Betty Crocker," she said, rolling her eyes. "Now I'm the chick hollerin' 'fuck that'!"

Laughing lightly, I shook my head. "You are a trip," I said.

"But it's a good ride." She smiled. "And don't worry. Everything is going to be fine. You're a bad bitch, sis, and bad bitches can't be stopped."

"Thanks, Trace," I said sincerely, "and thanks for the ride, boo," I said, kissing her cheek lightly. "Call me to let me know you made it home."

"Will do, boo," she smiled. "Love you, sis."

"Love you too."

*****

Five minutes later, I sat on my sofa trying to figure out my next move. I knew if Elena was coming for me, I had better have one, and I had to make it good. I was massaging my temples, trying hard to fight off the onset of a headache when my phone rang. "That was quick," I answered without looking at the caller ID.

"You act like you can't return your mother's calls!" The sound of my mama's voice sent my spirits straight down to my toes.

"I've been busy," I said bluntly.

"How is the job going?"

"It's going well," I said impatiently. I did a mental countdown, waiting for the real reason behind her phone call to be exposed.

"Good," she said blandly. "When is payday? I need you to send me some money."

"What happened to *your* job?"

"I got laid off," she said lowly.

I knew my mama getting "laid off" meant she was fired—again. In my twenty-three years of life, I never knew my mama to hold a job longer than three months. She was a repeat offender; always calling off or showing up late. Grams said she told my father the first time she met my mother that she wasn't about shit. My mama had yet to prove Grams wrong.

"Go get another one," I said. "I have my own bills I have to take care of whenever I get paid."

"Well, have you talked to your grandma?"

"Not this week," I said, hoping everything was fine with Grams. "Is she alright?" I asked, concerned.

"Oh, she gets all the fucking sympathy," she snapped, "and I don't get shit!"

"Is she alright?" I exhaled softly. I was not in the mood for mama's drama.

"She's fine," she snapped.

I exhaled gratefully.

"But you need to call her."

"I will call her tomorrow," I said, relieved.

"When you talk to her, ask her for $200," mama ordered. "Then put some money in my account."

"I'll see what I can do," I lied.

"Good, baby," she said sweetly. "Mama loves you."

"You too," I said dryly. I hung up without saying goodbye. *I refuse to end up like her*, I thought to myself. I had to rise to the top by any and all means necessary.

Thoughts of my grandmother ran through my head. I missed her terribly, so I decided to call just to hear her voice. After I filled her in on how my new job was going, leaving out the part where I lied to get it, I promised her I would come to visit as soon as I could. I also begged her not to give my mama a dime if she called.

Chapter 6

I strolled down the aisle of the marketing department on the third floor, pushing the rolling metal mail cart with a smile on my face and a little added twist in my hips. It was the beginning of a new day, and I had a brand new attitude. I looked and felt unbelievably sexy in my above-the-knee DKNY fitted skirt and five-inch stilettos. I was in the game, and I was determined to win. I still didn't know how far Elena had gone with her verification, but I was trying not to think about that. I was on mail duty again, but I chose not to look at it as punishment. Rather, I embraced the opportunity to meet more G&L associates and to see if there was any gossip floating around about me.

I captured the attention and turned the heads of several of my hopefully would-be co-workers as I made my rounds. To my delight, each of them seemed genuinely happy to see me, and Elena had yet to call me into her office.

I reached the end of the aisle and spotted Jamel sitting in one of the eight cubicles located in the middle of the floor. He sat staring at the flat-screen monitor, whispering and talking with a another man. The man stood beside Jamel's chair, leaning on the desk looking at the screen. When Jamel saw me, he looked up the nodded in my direction. The man stood up straight and waved. I walked up to the two of them and smiled.

"How's it going, Asia?" Jamel asked, staring at me.

"It's good, Jamel," I said, looking at the other man. "And who are you?" I asked.

"Hello. I'm Adam Wales," the tall blond-haired man said as he extended his hand to me.

I gave his hand a firm shake and watched as his eyes traveled from mine to my breasts then back up again. Jamel looked from Adam to me, clearing his throat.

"It's nice to meet you, Adam." I smiled sweetly.

Adam had emerald-green eyes and a nicely toned physique. His head was completely bald, and his face was hairless with the exception of a well-trimmed mustache. He was cute and didn't come off as cocky by any means. I figured Jamel was just pissed that he had to work side by side with a man who was equally confident and attractive.

"The pleasure is truly mine," Adam said, flashing a smile.

"Are the two of you working hard?" I asked, looking from one man to the other.

"Just going over some ideas I have for my ad pitch," Jamel said proudly. "Mr. Wales is critiquing the presentation for me."

"Well, I'm sure the best *woman* will win," I said confidently.

"Or man," Adam said.

Batting my eyes at him seductively I smiled. "I said it right the first time," I said. "Well, duty calls. Catch you later, Jamel. Nice to meet you, Adam." I sauntered off with my head held high and a smile on my face.

*****

Although Nathaniel allowed us the last four hours of our work day to work on our presentations, I needed a little extra time to prepare for mine. I no longer had a computer at home due to pawning my laptop, so I decided to stay late at the office and finish up my presentation in the G&L library. The idea I came up with was not only hot, but ultra-sexy. The problem I was having was putting it together on paper. I chalked my lack of focus up to the thoughts running through my head about my money woes and the problem Elena was becoming. I decided to call it a night and start fresh the next morning.

I was walking out of the library with my work in hand, when I practically stumbled into Jamel. "What are you still doing here?" he asked, staring at me suspiciously.

"Working on my presentation," I yawned lightly. "Why are you here?" I asked, curious.

"Left my cell phone upstairs," he said, stumbling over his words. "I was just about to go grab it."

For the first time since I'd met Jamel, he actually seemed nervous and unsure of himself. I didn't understand why, and at that moment, I really didn't care. The only thing on my mind was going home and taking a long, hot bath. "Well, I better get going," I said. "See you tomorrow."

"Have a good night, Asia," Jamel said quickly, practically sighing with relief that I was leaving.

This sent my radar completely up. I walked down the aisle toward the main entrance of G&L, waiting until I heard the elevator doors close. Once I was confident Jamel was well on his way up to the third floor, I did a 360.

* * * * *

Standing outside the office door, I peered through the blinds like a peeping Tom. I felt a rush of joy from my discovery, but at the same time, it was hard as hell for me to keep my lunch from coming back up my throat. Jamel stood with his pants and boxers around his ankles, a look of sheer pleasure, as he pumped what had to be at least nine hard inches in and out, in and out on a mission to bust a nut. After capturing the intimate moment with the camera on my cell phone, I slowly eased away from the window and out the main doors. Shaking my head, I laughed lightly as I sent the pictures to my own personal email address. I was about to knock Elena's big ass down off her high horse! I tapped my feet lightly while waiting for the elevator to come up.

"Miss Turner?"

Spinning around on my heels, I jumped at the sound of her voice. "Elena?" I said, throwing my hand up to my chest. "You startled me."

"I'm sure," she said, crossing her arms across her breasts. "What exactly are you doing here?" she questioned.

"I was working in the library," I said, waving my folder in the air. "I'm leaving now."

"If I remember correctly, the library is located on the first floor." Elena frowned.

"You're correct," I said sweetly. "I had some other things to attend to as well, but now I'm leaving."

"I don't know what you're up to ," she said sourly, "but I'm on to you."

I couldn't suppress my laughter. I was seconds away from busting Elena. I could taste the revenge on the tip of my tongue, and it was one of the sweetest things I ever tasted. "You're on to me?" I asked sarcastically. "Riddle me this, Elena," I continued, "what exactly are *you* doing here?"

"I was wrapping up some last-minute work," she said calmly. "When I noticed Mr. Harston's vehicle still in the parking lot, I wanted to make sure he was okay."

"Sure you did," I chuckled. "Did you find him?"

"I'm right here," Jamel said, coming down the corridor. He looked from me to Elena, then nervously back to me. "Just...just forgot my phone," he stuttered.

Elena adjusted her glasses and then shifted her weight from one leg to the other.

Guilty asses, I thought to myself, but I decided not to expose their little secret just yet. First, I had to make sure all the cards in the deck were going to fall in my favor. "There you go, Elena," I said, crossing my arms across my breasts.

"Jamel's just fine."

When the doors to the elevator opened, I immediately stepped on, followed by Jamel and then Elena. The three of us rode down in silence. I imagined the silence was uncomfortable for the two of them, but I was smiling brightly. Flipping my phone open, I glanced at the picture I had taken. The ball was officially back in my court.

Chapter 7

Easing down in the chair next to Jamel, I smiled seductively. The two of us were alone in the first floor break room. I knew Jamel sat in the break room every morning before training to read the daily paper, and I decided this was the perfect opportunity for me to approach him. "Good morning," I said sweetly.

"Good morning to you too," he said, clearing his throat. "How are you this morning?" he asked, placing his paper on the table. "What's with you this morning?" he asked cautiously.

"What do you mean?" I asked, trying to sound innocent.

"Why are you being so nice?"

"I'm in a very, very good mood this morning." It was true; I felt like a heavyweight who had just knocked out their opponent in the ring in the first round. Massaging his crotch gently with one hand, I stroked his cheek gently with the other.

Jamel looked confused and slightly taken aback from my display of affection.

"Am I making you uncomfortable?" I asked, lowering

my eyes.

"Shit, no, not at all," Jamel said, laughing lightly. "But you keep playing, and Ima have to find a corner to bend that ass over."

Squeezing the slowly developing growth in between his legs, I licked my lips. "Mmm," I moaned lowly. "Sounds nice, but first I want to ask you something."

"What's that?" he moaned lightly while I massaged in between his legs slowly.

Flickering my tongue along the edge of his earlobe, I whispered, "Do you think Adam will mind?"

"What?"

"Adam," I said, pulling my hand from his lap. Relaxing in my chair, I cocked my head to the side. "Or was he just a one-night stand?" I asked, giving him a sly smile.

"What are you talking about?" Jamel asked, straightening his tie. His eyes told me he knew I was aware of his alternative lifestyle, but he wasn't going to confess to anything.

Flipping my phone out, I scrolled to the pictures I had taken of him screwing Adam in the ass the night before. I placed the phone on the table and watched as Jamel scrolled through the photos.

"I knew there was something about you," I giggled, "something I just couldn't put my finger on. Now I know what it is!" I lowered my voice to prevent the associates that had entered the break room from hearing me. "You're just like me," I whispered. "You like dick."

Jamel looked like he had seen a ghost. The warm color seemed to vanish, and instantly his skin was pale. "No one will ever believe that I'm—"

"Gay?" I said, finishing his sentence. "They will when they see these," I said, holding up my cell phone.

"You can't tell anyone about this," Jamel ordered.

"Actually, I can," I corrected him. "But I won't as long as you're willing to give me your full cooperation."

"Cooperate how?"

*****

"I won't do it," Jamel said firmly.

After I briefed him on what I expected of him, he stood firm on his decision not to participate in my plan.

"Fine," I said. "Then get ready for everyone to get a peek of yours and Adam's lil' gay porn."

"This is blackmail," Jamel said sternly.

"No, sweetie, this is you scratching my back and me keeping your dirty little secret," I advised him. "Think about it. Imagine how Minister Harston would feel hearing that his son favors men." I was only making a threat to expose Jamel, but if he tried to defy my wishes, I would have put him on blast in front of the entire congregation. "What would Daddy's congregation say," I asked, "if they saw pictures of you and Adam plastered on the church bulletin board?"

"What if I talk to Elena and try to keep her off your back?" he suggested.

"Perfect. Then she'll come even harder because the object of her affection—meaning you—would be defending the woman she hates so much. That will never work," I said. "It's my way only."

"What if someone finds out?" he said. "Elena could lose her job."

"No one will ever know," I said sweetly. "Just play your part, and we will all be fine." I had no intentions of telling Jamel that I was going to personally ensure Elena was terminated. My desire to have her fired was a personal vendetta. That jealous bitch had treated me like shit from the moment she met me. She had the first laugh, but I was about to teach her that the baddest chick gets the last laugh, and I would soon be doubling over with laughter.

Chapter 8

Saturday, Tracey invited me over to a gathering she and Harold were having at their home. I wasn't in the mood for socializing, but I needed to get out of the house. Plus, Tracey wasn't about to take "no" for an answer. Tracey and Harold lived in a gated community called The River Club, an upscale community in Suwanee, just outside northern Atlanta. On the rare occasions when I visited Tracey at her home, I felt like I was stepping into another world, a world where elegance, class, and serenity came together all tied up with a million-dollar bow. Most of the homes in The River Club were worth more than a million dollars, and Tracey's home was no exception. Valued at a stunning one and a half million, the home had all the luxuries of a five-star hotel and then some. Harold had purchased the home before he met Tracey, and looking at the six-bedroom, eight-bath masterpiece, it was easy to see that Harold was a man who knew how to appreciate the finer things in life.

"Harold invited a few of his associates," Tracey informed me as she pulled into the three-car garage.

She had been quiet for the majority of the drive to her home. When I asked if everything was okay, she said she was fine and tried to make a joke or two, but I knew my best friend like the stars know the sky, and I could always tell when she was holding something back. I decided not to push her and knew whatever was bothering her would eventually come out.

"What are they like?" I asked,

"Boring, rich, and fake."

"It's a good thing you have me here," I said, checking out my appearance in her car mirror. I had chosen to wear my Dior dress because it was sexy and classy. To complete my ensemble, I wore a pair of five-inch stilettos that strapped around my ankles. I wore my hair down with loose curls bouncing at my shoulders. I felt and looked sexy.

"Why do you think I insisted that you come?" she asked, shifting the car into park. "Hell, I need at least one real person on deck that I can trust."

"You do have your hubby," I reminded her.

"Like I said, I need at least one person on deck I can *trust*," she said solemnly.

"What's up?" I asked. "Seriously, are you and Harold having problems?"

She rolled her eyes then shook her head. "Naw, I'm just frustrated," she said. "It's just amazing how he bitches me out about spending money, but then his ass goes all out for a bunch of lames who couldn't care less if he lives or dies."

My instinct was telling me the brunt of their problems had nothing to do with the budget Harold had placed on their household, nor did it involve the party he had chosen to throw. I knew there was more to it than that, but I wasn't the type to push a person into sharing with me. Instead, I took what Tracey told me and tried to lighten her mood. "Girl, you know men like to showcase for their so-called friends," I said lightly. "Don't stress over that bullshit. At the end of the day, you're the queen, and what the queen says goes. I guarantee if you start rationing the coochie, he will forget all about a damn budget," I added.

"Maybe," she said, laughing as she opened the driver's side door. "Or maybe not," I heard her mumble.

* * * * *

Sipping on my glass of Krug Rose, I watched as Harold and Tracey worked the room, making small talk with their guests. Together, they looked like a beautiful power couple. Tracey wore a short red silk dress that dipped low in the front, with open-toe stilettos, while Harold rocked a red button-front shirt and tailored black slacks. The two of them complimented each other perfectly. Although Harold was twelve years Tracey's senior, he could easily pass for twenty-three. He stood six-two with pecan-colored skin, and he had low-cut hair without a hint of gray, sitting atop an athletic build. He was handsome in his own right, but standing side by side with my beautiful friend made him look gorgeous.

After smiling and nodding in agreement with practically every word Harold said, Tracey excused herself from the small crowd Harold was entertaining and joined me. "Girl, let's go out on the terrace and relax," she said, exhaling. "The air is thick with bullshit in here."

Laughing lightly, I nodded my head while following Tracey through the crowd.

Once the two of us were settled on her terrace, she began to vent. "Did you see the skinny red bone with the three-sizes-too-small dress and four-sizes-too-big titties?"

"Yes," I laughed. "A damn mess."

"Her name is Christina, and you can't tell the bitch she ain't fine."

"What's your issue with her?"

"She likes to stand a little too close to my hubby," she said. I watched as Tracey popped a small pill in her mouth. "Want one?"

"What is it?"

"Ecstasy," she said in a mellow voice, "a little something to keep me ready for my hubby and relax my mind."

"Trace, why you fucking with pills now?" I asked, more concerned than angry.

"I told you why," she mumbled, "and don't judge me. It's hard being me."

"I'm sure," I said, "but it'll be even harder being a strung-out version of you."

*****

Later I left Tracey napping on the terrace while I slipped into her office to utilize her laptop. I had to get my presentation together, and I knew it was my last opportunity to do so before it was time to present it. I was halfway down the hall to the office when I heard low moans coming from one of the spare bedrooms. Following the sounds, I stopped at the door and peeked through the small opening. Inside, I saw Harold with his hands cupping Christina's ass and his tongue probing her mouth. My first thought was to march out and get my bestie, but then I thought of her current condition. I made the decision to keep quiet for the moment, but not before slamming the door shut to let them know someone had witnessed their private show.

Chapter 9

After presenting my ad pitch, I sat in the conference room watching Jamel as he presented his idea for the Juicy Couture campaign. I felt secure that I had a made a good impression on Nathaniel and the members of management in the room. Jamel also looked confident as he spoke in front of them, but his presentation was a mess. He was rambling on and on and had completely forgotten about his target audience. It was obvious at that moment that Jamel didn't have a clue what he was doing. The truth was that even before Jamel opened his mouth to speak, I had no fear that he would outshine me. He hadn't proven me wrong, and a part of me wondered if his lack of focus was due to the fact that he was too busy trying to cover his ass and keep me happy by cozying up to Elena. I know having Jamel seduce Elena might seem a little extreme. However, it wasn't any different from the ass-kissing he did to get his internship in the first place, as far as I was concerned. The only difference was that he now had to put his dick where his mouth was.

Bethany, on the other hand, came hard. She was articulate and confident, and she killed it with her presentation. When Nathaniel announced that Bethany would be the one having lunch with Parker, I was disappointed but not at all surprised.

I didn't want to portray myself as a sore loser or a hater, so as everyone was clearing the room, I walked up to Bethany to congratulate her. "Your presentation was hot," I said sincerely. "Congratulations."

"Thanks, Asia." Bethany smiled, flashing her blue eyes at me. "And sorry."

"Sorry about what?" I asked. I was truly clueless as to why she was offering me an apology.

"Maybe you'll have better luck with the next assignment," she said, running her fingers though her hair. "I mean, they can't get any worse for you. First mail duty, then..." She didn't finish her sentence. Instead, she lowered her eyes at me. Her face held an expression that screamed at me, *"I pity you!"*

"Then what?"

"Then today," she said lowly while shaking her head. "It really wasn't fair for them to put you up against me."

"We both hold the same position in this company at this time," I said, placing my hand on my hip, "so the competition is fair. It just so happens that you won *this* time." I wanted to add, *"So don't get grand, bitch!"* but I decided against it.

"Anyone with a thorough history of advertising would be able to see the loops and weaknesses in your pitch," she said sarcastically. "This is the major leagues, and what you just presented was a tee ball."

No she didn't! I thought. Bethany was standing in my face and belittling me and my work.

"Parker Bryant may know your name," she added, "but after he has lunch with me, he will see I'm the right one for the job. But you should look on the bright side," she said. "It could have been worse. You could be Jamel." She gave me a small smirk then stepped around me and exited the room.

Under different circumstances, I probably would have respected the fact that she was bold enough to say the things she was saying to my face, but this was not a normal circumstance. Bethany had officially sat on me while at the same time making the top of my shit list.

*****

I was in a funk for the rest of the morning and couldn't wait until the day was over. It was obvious that Bethany was the superstar for the day and enjoying every moment of the limelight. She was flying high and pushing my buttons with every flap of her wings.

For lunch, I decided to relieve some stress in the company gym. I breathed heavily as sweat trickled slowly down my face. Pumping my arms fiercely, I walked quickly on the treadmill. It had been months since I had worked out, and my body was crying for me to stop, but I pushed myself on. I ran out of sheer frustration and anger. When I finally felt like my legs might give out, I began to slow my pace in an effort to bring my heart rate down. I was almost back to my normal breathing.

I was so in gulfed in my run that I hadn't noticed Bethany coming through the door. I looked up and saw her walking out of the ladies' locker room wearing spandex shorts and a fitted crop top, carrying a small Nike gym bag in hand. In that outfit, she looked one skipped meal away from being anorexic. "Asia!" she chanted, "I didn't know you used this gym."

"I did today," I said, breathing deeply. I picked up the towel I had been using and dabbed at my face lightly.

"I make time every day to work out," she said. "Exercise is great for the body."

Looking at her thin frame, I laughed. "So is eating," I said sarcastically.

Batting her eyes at me, Bethany smiled. "I plan to eat good tomorrow," she said slyly. Her tone was sweet, but her demeanor told me she was being slick. "I'll be sure and let you and Jamel know how it feels to dine on the fifth floor." Bethany dropped her gym bag on the floor behind the machine located next to the one I was on and then stepped on.

Taking a gulp of my bottled water, I cut my eyes in her direction. I was beyond the point of being fed up with her. "Thanks for the heads up," I said. "It'll let me know what I have to look forward to once I get my office next to Parker's."

Jogging slowly on the belt of the treadmill, Bethany

laughed. "I guess if you're going to wish," she said, "you should make it big."

Grabbing my towel, I stepped of the treadmill with my water in hand. "I don't make wishes, Bethany," I said sweetly. "I make things happen." I marched off to the dressing room, biting my tongue every step of the way. If the two of us had not been on company property, I would have given Bethany a well-whooped ass. Instead, I decided to help her fall on it. Slipping in the locker room, I pulled my gym bag and purse from the metal locker I had been using while in the gym. After retrieving two fresh bottles of water from the Coke machine, I slipped in the ladies' bathroom and removed the small plastic bag I had retrieved from Tracey's house over the weekend. I twisted the plastic top off one of the bottles and dropped two of the ecstasy pills in. I secured the top back on the bottle and slipped back in the gym. "Here you go, Bethany," I said, walking up to the treadmill where Bethany was engaged in a full sprint. "A peace offering," I said, turning the top on the unopened bottle.

Looking over at me, Bethany smiled. "Peace offering?" she asked breathing heavily.

I watched as she slowed her pace back down to a jog. "Yes, the best woman won today," I said gloomily. "I respect that." I reopened the second bottle and offered it to her.

"Thank you, Asia!" She smiled victoriously. She came to a complete stop before taking the bottle from my hand,

and I watched as she guzzled half of it down. "Whew!" She exhaled. "That hit the spot."

"I bet," I said. "Well, let me go hit the shower."

"Thanks for the water, Asia," Bethany said affectionately.

"No thanks needed," I said, smirking lightly. "The pleasure is all mine." Bending down, I tied the laces of my shoe tightly and quickly dropped the plastic bag down inside the opening of Bethany's bag.

*****

I exited the locker room to find Bethany lying on the floor with Helena, the G&L trainer, kneeling next to her. Helena rubbed Bethany's arm gently while telling her that everything would be alright. Bethany's face was drenched in sweat, and there was a large red knot on her forehead.

"What happened?" I asked, running to Bethany's side.

"She tripped over her feet and then bumped her head," Helena explained.

"Your hands feel sooo good," Bethany squealed, laughing hysterically. "Don't stop."

Helena looked at me with raised eyebrows.

"Maybe she has a concussion," I suggested innocently, although I knew Bethany was high and trippin' from the pills I had slipped her.

"HEMSI is on their way," Helena said. "Just stay still."

"I'm f-i-i-i-i-ne," Bethany moaned, attempting to sit up, "but I am soo thirsty."

"Don't move!" Helena ordered. Helena attempted to wipe the sweat that was pouring from Bethany's face with her hand.

"That's her bag," I said cleverly, pointing to Bethany's gym bag. "Her towel's in there."

I watched as Helena dug through the contents of the bag until she found what I wanted her to see: the drugs I had planted on Bethany earlier. Holding the bag up Helena frowned.

"What's that?" I asked casually.

Staring at the little blue pills, Helena shook her head. "Bethany, did you take these?" Helena asked, ignoring me.

"I'm thirsty," she repeated, "and hot." She rubbed the knot on her head, which was now a grotesque shade of purple and black, and then she burst out laughing like a crazy ass.

* * * * *

"It's a good thing you were here when it happened," Nathaniel said to Helena, as the three of us stood outside the gym watching Bethany being carried out on a stretcher.

The scene after Bethany's fall was chaotic. Associates in the offices nearby rushed into the halls to see what was going on. Elena had rushed to the scene as well after security alerted her that there had been an accident.

Helena was the one to explain what she saw and what she found in Bethany's gym bag. "I'm happy to help," Helena said. "I just wish it was under different circumstances."

"I like Bethany," I lied softly. "I hope she's okay."

"I'm sure she'll be fine," Nathaniel said, looking at me. "Don't worry, Asia," he said, rubbing my shoulder gently.

I nodded my head in agreement.

Parker arrived on the scene just as the EMTs were pulling off. I could see the concern stamped across his face as he walked toward us. "Is everyone else alright?" he asked.

"Yes," Nathaniel replied.

"Were there any witnesses?" Parker asked.

"Helena witnessed the fall," Nathaniel informed him. "Asia was in the locker room at the time of the fall, but she did see what happened afterwards."

Looking at me, Parker nodded his head. "Nate, do me a favor and get everyone back in their offices."

"Sure," Nathaniel said

"Helena and Asia, I'd like to speak with the two of you in private," Parker said.

*****

After giving Parker the details of what I had witnessed after leaving the locker room. I listened as he explained the importance of discretion and privacy at G&L. "I can understand how easy it would be to share this kind of information with one of your peers," Parker continued, staring at me, "however, I'm asking you to please refrain from discussing what you witnessed today."

"You can trust me to keep what I saw today to myself," I said honestly.

"Thank you, Asia."

"Don't thank me yet," I said, leaning forward in my chair. "There is something I want in return."

Cocking his head to the side, Parker watched me carefully. "And what is that?" he asked.

Chapter 10

Parker agreed to my demands, which included him awarding me the lunch meeting that Bethany had unfortunately forfeited after taking a fall in the office and being caught with illegal drugs on the premises. I told her the best woman won that day, and it wasn't a lie; I was that woman. Sitting across from Parker in PF Chang's was an added bonus, and I was enjoying every minute of.

"How is the program going?" he asked.

"It's going well," I said. "I met some wonderful people in the company."

"And how is Nathaniel doing as an instructor?"

"Nathaniel is great." I smiled. "He's patient and down to Earth. My only complaint is that he dumped me in the mailroom." I was still smiling, even though I was venting.

Parker laughed lightly. "That was actually my doing," he confessed.

I was surprised and intrigued by that information. "Really?" I asked. "May I ask why?"

"I wanted to see how you would handle yourself," he said, clasping his hands together in front of him. "True stars know how to adapt and adjust. They take the hand they're dealt and turn it into a winning book."

I meditated on his words before responding. "How am I adapting thus far?" I asked, staring at him.

"So far, you've shown me you know how to handle change, and you're one hell of a negotiator."

"You're referring to this lunch?" I concluded.

"Yes," he said. "This is completely outside the norm."

I knew that normal lunch meetings were conducted at G&L in the executive dining room, but I had pushed the envelope and requested lunch outside the office. "Well, I'm not your normal woman," I said gently, "and you're not the average man."

"How do you know?" he asked. "I could be just another corporate suit."

"You are far from being just another corporate suit," I said seductively.

"Again," he said, "how do you know?"

"The average corporate suit would not be here with me right now."

There was silence between the two of us until our waiter returned with our meals.

I took my time savoring every bit of my almond and cashew chicken while Parker consumed the roasted duck he ordered. The two of us conversed lightly throughout our meal about the company and the goals Parker had set for the next year. Parker was driven and determined, an attractive quality in any man. He was also mysterious and at times a man of few words. This intrigued me and in some ways turned me on. Granted, he kept our communication strictly business, but I felt he was comfortable with me and willing to discuss any subject I placed before him.

"So are you married, single, or other?" I asked casually.

"Other," he said.

Please don't say gay, I thought.

"I'm, uh, in a relationship," he said.

"How long?"

"Five years," he said. "And yourself?" he asked.

Damn, I thought to myself. *Five years and no wedding bells?* It was obvious someone had a fear of real commitment. Looking across the table at Parker, I was willing to bet my paycheck that the someone was him. "Single as they come," I answered.

"Come on now," he said, frowning slightly. "There has to be a special someone in your life."

"Nope," I sighed. "I guess it's true what they say."

"What's that?" he asked.

"All the good ones are already spoken for," I flirted, referring to him.

Blushing slightly he smiled. "There is someone for everyone," he said, "and trust me, you will know when you find him."

* * * * *

Relaxing in the leather seat of the company limo, I stretched my legs out in front of me. I had chosen to wear my red wrap dress that stopped slightly above my knees and red open-toe heels because the dress hugged my body but still looked office appropriate. I was trying to fly under Elena's radar, and I didn't want to do or wear anything that would bring forth her unwanted attention—at least not until Jamel had delivered on his end of our agreement. Parker sat opposite of me checking his emails on his Blackberry. I knew that I needed to recapture his attention and capture it quickly. Easing my shoes off, I exhaled lightly while wiggling my toes. The expression on his face from my actions was indeed priceless.

"What?" I asked politely. "My feet stink?"

"No," he chuckled. "At least I don't think so."

"Whew," I said dramatically. "You had me worried."

He looked from my eyes to my toes and then back to my eyes again.

"You know you are a completely different woman from the one I found in tears that day in the waiting room," he said.

That's because I'm a good actress, I thought to myself. "Is that a good thing?" I asked.

"Yes," he said. "You're a lot stronger than I thought."

"And you are a lot more laidback than I thought," I said.

"Is that a good thing?"

"Yes, a very good thing," I said. "In the office you seem so uptight."

"I didn't get where I am by being everyone's friend," he said. "I got here through hard work, discipline, and dedication."

"You can be disciplined without being uptight," I told him. "Smile more often and laugh. Let your guard down just a little bit"

"When you let your guard down to the wrong individuals, it leaves you vulnerable and exposed," he stated emphatically.

"When you let it down for the right one, though, it can lead to pleasure and unimaginable victories," I said suggestively.

"Pleasure and business make a bad combination," he said smoothly.

"Do you really believe that?" I asked. "Or is that what's in the handbook?"

He didn't respond; he didn't have to. The tension between the two of us was thick as fog, and the attraction between the two of us was undeniable.

*****

I was headed to the training room when I ran into Jamel and Elena coming down the hall. Elena was all smiles until her eyes locked with mine. "Good afternoon, Jamel," I smiled. "Hello, Elena."

"How was your lunch, Asia?" Jamel asked, standing with his hands in his pockets.

"Delicious," I smiled, patting my stomach. "How was yours?"

"I didn't do anything special," he said, shrugging, "but I was in good company."

Elena's expression softened as the corner of her lips began to turn up into a smile. It pleased me that Jamel had that effect on her. I would be even more pleased once I had something in hand to bust Elena with.

"How is everything, Elena?" I asked sweetly.

"Everything is fine, *Miss* Turner," she said, putting emphasis on "Miss."

The three of us stood there caught in an awkward moment until Elena finally stated she had to get back to her office. I could sense she wanted me to leave so she and Jamel could continue their conversation in private.

Once she was gone, I turned to Jamel. "So did you get it?" I asked anxiously.

"Get what?"

"You know what," I said. "The damn draw's." Rolling my eyes, I exhaled. "Have you hit it yet?" I asked.

"No," he said quickly. "It ain't that simple, Asia."

"Yes the hell it is," I whispered. "She's a woman, and you're a man. She has the coochie, and you have a dick," I added. "Do the math."

Jamel looked annoyed and frustrated with me.

"You do have sex with women, right?" I asked hesitantly. "Or is it only men that get you aroused?"

"Yes, I like women," he snapped. "The problem is not that my dick can't get the job done. The problem is she's a virgin," he said. "She's saving herself for marriage."

I was speechless and a little amazed. "Isn't she like fifty?" I asked, shocked. I knew there were women still in the world saving themselves for their husbands, but I had never actually met one over the age of twenty-five.

"She's thirty-nine," Jamel corrected me.

"Yeah, whatever," I said, brushing off his attitude. "So, you're telling me you've gotten nowhere with her?" I asked. "That's basically what you're saying?"

He didn't answer.

"I knew better than to strike a deal with your gay ass," I said sarcastically. "You don't even know what team you want to play for."

"I'm keeping my end of the deal," he said, cutting his eyes at me. "You just better keep yours."

"Get me something to work with ASAP, and I will," I said firmly. "Otherwise, the deal's off, and I'm going straight to Daddy Dearest with those photos!"

Jamel's demeanor quickly changed at the mention of his father. "I got you," he said gently.

"You better have *you*," I threatened. "Now handle your damn business before I do."

"I'm working on it," he whined. "Hell, I know you see me around here talking to her."

That much was true. I also had to give him credit for knowing the tidbit of information about Elena's sex life or lack thereof. It was obvious he was doing something right and had the woman opening up—even if it wasn't below the waist. "What else have you learned?" I asked calmly.

Chapter 11

The fifth floor, also known as the Executive Floor, at G&L was without a doubt the most luxurious floor in the building. Unlike the Ad Sales and Marketing floors, where there were lots of cubicles and shared work-spaces, each associate on the fifth floor had their own private offices.

I pulled the glass doors open with Parker's name on them and stepped inside. Parker's office was the biggest in the building. It even had its own waiting room and receptionist area. Inside the room was a small waiting area with a couple of cushioned folding chairs and a nice wooden L-shaped receptionist desk with a leather high-back chair, a PC with a flat-screen monitor, and a multi-line phone. The phone was ringing loudly with multiple lines lit up. Jamel had advised me that Parker's normal assistant was going to be out of the office on medical leave and Elena was stressing to get someone to fill in, so I decided to pay him a visit just to see if I could find a window of opportunity.

As I approached the closed wooden door inside the room, I could hear Parker speaking to Elena on speakerphone. "I'm trying to find a temp right now," I heard Elena say over the intercom. "I've called the staffing company, and they are going to send over someone as soon as they pull resumes. In the meantime, I'll try to see if I can get someone up there to answer your calls," I heard her say.

"Thanks, Elena. Just do what you can," Parker sounded frustrated but was still polite.

It was in that moment that I saw the window of opportunity swing open. Plopping down in the leather chair, I went to work. "Parker Bryant's office. Can you hold?" I answered the first line. "Parker Bryant's office. How may I help you? I'm sorry, but he's presently in a meeting." I told the man on the second line. "I do apologize for the inconvenience, but he will be more than happy to call you back." Grabbing the message pad and pen lying on the desk, I scribbled down the man's name and number. "Thank you so much," I smiled. "Have a great day. I'll be sure to give him the message," I said politely into the phone. "Thank you for calling, and have a great day."

By the time I had retrieved the next call and taken a message, Parker was standing beside me.

"Good morning," I smiled, handing him the message slips.

"Good morning, Asia." The expression on his face was a mixture of relief and confusion. "Thank you," he said, reading the messages.

"You're very welcome."

"Did Elena send you?" he asked. His soft brown eyes

seemed to light up at the question.

"No." I laughed lightly. "I was actually passing by and decided to stop in and say hello, when I heard your phone ringing off the hook."

"And you decided to jump right in?" His eyes narrowed slightly as he folded his arms across his chest.

"You don't mind, do you?" I stood and stepped back from the desk. His expression was unreadable, and I was beginning to think my interfering was not the best thing to do.

"No, not at all," he said before exhaling slowly. "Thank you." He smiled slightly. "Thank you."

Smiling, I nodded my head. "You're welcome," I said, walking back toward the door. "Well, I should get back downstairs now. I was just on break and decided to stop in and see you." I moved slowly, waiting for him to say something, anything, inviting me to stay, but he didn't. I was halfway out the door when the phone began to ring again.

"Asia!"

The sound of Parker's voice stopped me in my tracks. Turning on my heels, I smiled. "Yes?"

"I really could use your help."

* * * * *

To say that Parker needed my help would be an understatement. For the first two hours, his phone rang constantly, and the door to his office was constantly opening and closing from clients and associates entering and exiting. However, after lunch, things seemed to calm down, and I found myself sitting and waiting for the next phone call to come in.

Parker had been confined to his office until he finally exited carrying his Blackberry and car keys. "I have to make a quick run," he said, looking at me. "I'll be back in about forty minutes. If you have any problems call my cell. The number is on speed dial, Number 3. A woman by the name of Sarah is going to come in to see me around one thirty," he advised. "She's with the staffing agency. I may be running a few minutes late, so if you don't mind, just ask her to wait for me."

"Sure," I smiled, nodding my head. "Is there anything else you'd like for me to do while you're gone?" I asked.

"That's it." He smiled, hurrying toward the door. "Thank you, Asia."

As soon as Parker was gone, I flipped out my cell phone and dialed Tracey. "Guess where I am," I said excitedly.

"No time for guessing. Just tell me."

"In the office of the CEO," I said, reclining in my chair.

"What!?" Tracey squealed loudly.

"You heard me," I said, sucking my teeth.

"That's what I'm talking 'bout, A!" Tracey cheered. "Fuck an internship. Go straight to the top!"

"Calm down," I told her. "I'm only filling in for his assistant for a few hours," I said, spinning around in my chair. "He's expecting a temp to come in for the rest of the day." I sighed.

"So what?"

"So it's back to the training room."

"So why are you going back? " Tracey asked. "Shit, you're already there," she stated, reminding me of the obvious. "Move in for the kill. But look, sis, I gotta go," she said quickly. "Believe it or not, Harold had the nerve to schedule a showing for me."

"The nerve of him," I teased.

"I know!" she exclaimed. "I'm telling you my hubby is on some more shit, A. As soon as I discover what it is, there is going to be trouble."

Flashbacks of Harold cozying up to Christina at their party ran through my mind. I still felt guilty for not telling Tracey what I had witnessed, but I just couldn't break the news to her. "I'm sure it's nothing," I said, faking a light laugh.

"It better be nothing," she said smacking her lips. "Bye, sis."

"Bye, Trace."

I was 65 percent sure my assisting Parker in his time of need and showing a willingness to work in the mailroom would be more than enough to show that I was willing to work hard and help out whenever and wherever needed and that it would be enough to land me a permanent position. However, 65 percent isn't shit when the odds are stacked against you. You need a 100 percent guarantee. That's why when the heavyset, conservatively dressed redhead pushed the doors to Parker's office open and announced to me that her name was Sarah , I politely thanked her for coming and informed her the position had already been filled.

*****

"Welcome back," I smiled as Parker walked through the doors of the waiting room.

His face was set hard with an expression that told me his errands hadn't gone well. "Thank you, Asia," he said flatly. "Do I have any messages?"

Handing him the few messages I had taken while he was gone, I contemplated on whether or not to address what he was thinking. I decided to wait.

"Didn't that Sarah show?" he asked, walking toward his office door.

"No, no she didn't."

"Figures," he exhaled loudly. "Get Elena on the phone, please, and let her know."

I watched him as he walked into his office and slammed the door. Calling Elena was not an option, considering I had lied to Sarah about the position. I decided to try my luck at getting Parker to open up to me. After knocking lightly on his door, I smoothed my hands over my skirt and adjusted my jacket.

"Come in."

Walking into Parker's office, I took a deep breath and exhaled softly.

Parker sat behind the huge mahogany desk, staring at the flat-screen monitor in front of him. "Yes, Asia?" He continued to stare at the screen as he spoke to me.

"Would you like to talk about it?"

"Talk about what?"

"Whatever it is that's bothering you."

"I'm fine," he said, continuing to stare at the screen.

"Are you sure?"

"Positive," he mumbled. "Thank you for asking."

"Would you like me to stay and assist you for the rest of the day?"

"That will be fine."

"Is there anything I can help you with right now?"

"Not at this time, but hold all my calls."

"No problem," I said, staring at him while wondering what was so intriguing on the screen in front of him. I was happy with his response to my working with him, but his failure to make eye contact was beginning to get under my skin. I didn't give a damn if he was staring at the solution for world peace on the screen, I was raised to think that when someone is speaking to you, you look them in their eyes. "Do you realize how rude that is?" I finally asked.

"What?"

"You're speaking to me without looking at me," I stated. "That's rude."

Looking up, Parker gazed at me with raised eyebrows. "It's a habit."

"Is it?"

"Yes."

"To make this afternoon the best possible," I spoke, staring into his eyes, "let's both try to get rid of our bad habits."

I could tell he was caught off guard by my statement.

Rubbing his hands together, he cocked his head to the side while continuing to stare at me. There was silence between us until he finally nodded his head and said, "I'll try to remember that."

"Thank you," I said before strolling out the office door.

The rest of the afternoon went extremely well. I could still sense that something was wrong with Parker, but he forced a smile whenever he asked me to do something, and each time he spoke to me he looked me directly in the eyes. A couple of times I heard him talking on his Blackberry to someone, and I heard him call her "baby." From what I could decipher, the conversation was somewhat heated. My intuition told me that "baby" was the woman he was in a relationship with, and she may have played a big part in his change of attitude when he returned to the office.

Elena hadn't called to check on Sarah, which was a plus for me. I knew there would be consequences and repercussions for my actions, but at that moment, I really didn't give a damn.

After an hour of peace and quiet in the office, I decided to approach Parker again. "Are you feeling better?" I asked, standing in front of his desk.

Drumming his fingers on the desk he nodded his head. "I'm fine," he said. "Really I am."

"Famous last words," I said, even though I couldn't remember where I'd heard the phrase before.

"For some," he said. "For me, they're true."

"This is what I was referring to," I told him.

"What do you mean?"

"In the limo," I said. "Uptight."

"What do you suggest I do?" he asked, leaning forward in his chair. "Kick off my shoes and wiggle my toes?"

It was hard for me to tell if he was being sarcastic or not, so I decided to make light of his statement. "Only if your feet don't stink," I said, light-heartedly. "Right now I'm not willing to take that chance. So take off your jacket," I said, walking around to the side of his desk.

"For what?"

"Because I asked nicely," I said, exhaling lightly. "Please take off your jacket."

For a second, Parker looked like he was contemplating refusing. Finally, he stood and removed his jacket.

"Sit down," I ordered. I waited until he was seated before walking up behind the chair. Running my hands over his shoulder blades, I felt the well-developed muscles underneath his cotton shirt. Kneading his shoulder blades gently, I waited for Parker to protest. When he didn't, I slid in, digging my fingers as far in as his clothing would allow them to go. "Close your eyes," I whispered.

"Asia—"

Pressing my finger to his lips, I silenced him. "Close your eyes," I said.

Parker did as I ordered.

"Relax, "I said. "Take a deep a breath in through your nose." Rubbing his tension filled shoulders I continued to speak softly. "Exhale slowly through your lips."

The sound of Parker breathing in and out slowly began to excite me.

"Focus on peace and pleasure," I whispered, stroking the side of his neck gently. Reaching around to the front of his collar, I slowly unbuttoned his collar from around his neck.

Relaxing in the chair, Parker exhaled softly.

I slid my hands down over his pecs, I continued to unbutton his shirt until I reached the top of his pants. Underneath his shirt, Parker wore a t-shirt, and rubbing his chest gently, I admired the flawless brown skin peeking from underneath the thin fabric. Squeezing his defined pecs, I whispered, "Feel good?"

"Yes," he moaned.

Inside my panties, my pussy began to purr. I was desperately trying to ignore her cry for love while trying to resist my urge to slip my fingers further down Parker's body. Grabbing his neck gently, I guided his head back until his lips were in the perfect position for me to lean down and press mine to his. I could feel his warm breath against my face as I leaned over, contemplating my next move.

Slowly opening his eyes, Parker stared up at me. Cuffing my wrist softly with his hand, he guided me until I was standing beside him. He eased the chair back, allowing me enough room to stand between him and the desk. Staring in his warm eyes, I stroked his face slowly. He leaned his face into the palm of my hand, pressing his lips against my skin. It felt like there was a small river pushing in between my legs, slowly trickling out. I was wet and ready. Easing out of the chair, Parker stood over me. I could see in his eyes that he wanted me, and if the thirst in his eyes wasn't enough, the hardness poking through his pants was. Cradling my face in his warm hands, Parker bent down until our lips were a breath away from being one.

My mouth watered from the anticipation until he hesitated. "No," he whispered, stepping back. Backing away slowly, Parker ran his hands across his head before slipping into his private restroom.

Ain't that some shit? I snapped to myself.

* * * * *

"I hope I didn't drive you too crazy today." Parker smiled as the two of us exited the elevator. It was six o'clock, and we were finally ready to leave the office.

"Working with you is a piece of cake." I smiled. *It's the sexual frustration that's killing me*, I thought.

"You say that now," he said seriously, "but let's see how you feel at the end of this week."

I didn't want to make any assumptions about what he was saying, so I asked just for confirmation. "Does this mean I will have the pleasure of working with you for the rest of the week?"

"It does," he said.

I was so happy I felt like doing cartwheels out the front door of the building, but I chose to refrain. Instead I smiled and said, "I'll see you in the morning."

"Have a good evening, Asia," he said, holding the door open for me.

"You too."

Tracey was parked in front of the building, waiting for me. I barely had time to close the passenger side door of her BMW before she started grilling me about Parker. "Tell me that ain't him!" she stated as we watched Parker slide behind the wheel of a midnight-blue Ferrari California.

"Who?"

"Mr. CEO, that's who!"

"Yeah, that's him."

"That mofo is fiiine!" she blurted out, staring at me.

"That he is," I said.

Tracey looked at me with her mouth opened wide. "The two of you doing a lil' somethin' somethin'?"

"No, just work," I said, staring out the window.

"You're a good one," she said. "I don't know if I could do it." Tracey continued to ramble on about Parker and then transitioned into complaints about her husband.

I nodded in agreement while thinking about everything that could have gone down with Parker when the two of us were alone earlier. Something told me the next time the opportunity presented itself, he wouldn't resist the obvious urge he felt.

Chapter 12

According to Oscar, the word throughout the office was that Adam was strongly pushing Jamel to be selected for the department opening. This tidbit of information didn't surprise me. I assumed Jamel was still tapping Adam's ass, and from the look on Adam's face the night I had seen them together, I would say Adam was enjoying every inch of it. Bethany was a distant memory, and although everyone knew she was no longer with the company, I was the only one who truly knew the real reason.

It was easy to see why Parker was the man in charge at G&L. He had a way of demonstrating his power without obvious force. He could take his own ideas or thoughts and present them in a way that made everyone forget anything and everything they had planned before. I loved working with him, and I was absorbing his knowledge like a sponge. The two of us had shared moments of silent eye contact but had yet to have another encounter. This would soon change.

Knocking on his office door, I looked at my reflection in

the waiting room window. I looked fabulous in my body-hugging black ruffled-collar sleeveless dress and leopard print open-toe stilettos. I wore a wide black belt, which only further accentuated my small waist and wide hips. I'd taken an extra fifteen minutes on my hair, and the end result was a bounty of big curls that fell over my shoulders.

"Come in"

"Good morning." I smiled sweetly, walking through Parker's office door.

He sat behind his desk staring at his computer monitor. He was wearing a black pin-striped suit with a black silk tie. "Good morning," he spoke as he slowly pulled his eyes from his monitor. He paused for a millisecond as he looked at me and then asked, "How are you today?"

"I'm fine," I said, slowly walking over to his desk and easing down in the chair directly across from him. "How are you this morning?" I asked, crossing my legs slowly.

"I'm fine, thank you," Parker said, looking me directly in the eyes. I waited for his eyes to travel to my breasts, legs, or anywhere on my body, but they never did.

"Can I get you anything?" I asked, lowering my eyes.

"Coffee would be nice," he said. "Also, can you send Jessica some get well flowers?" he asked.

"Of course I can," I said. "That's sweet of you."

"She's a wonderful assistant," he said. "I would be lost without her."

"Are you lost now?" I asked, pretending to be offended.

"Of course not," he said. "I was just—"

"I know," I said, cutting him off. "I know what you meant."

"Good."

"Besides, after having a taste of me," I said sensually, "uh...correction, of my work, Jessica will have some mighty large shoes to fill."

Leaning back in his chair, Parker rubbed his chin while shaking his head. "I'll keep that in mind," he said.

"Be right back." I smiled, standing, then turned my back to him. Spinning back around on my heels, I looked at him. "Cream? Sugar?" I asked, lowering my voice seductively.

"Both."

Walking over to the edge of his desk, I leaned forward. "Well, what are you waiting for?" I asked, batting my eyes. "You said you wanted cream and sugar."

"Asia," he said, shaking his head.

"Oh, you meant for the coffee," I said, winking my eye. "Be right back." The two of us stared at each other in silence until I finally turned and left the office.

* * * * *

"How you doing?" Jamel asked, standing next to me. He had a smile on his face that looked like it could stretch the length of a football field. The two of us stood in the break room in front of one of three coffeemakers. I had just finished preparing Parker's coffee when Jamel walked up dressed in a gorgeous tailored suit. The emerald-green in the suit complimented his skin beautifully. I'll admit he looked good, but I would never have admitted that to him.

"I'm good."

Jamel crossed his arms across his chest as his eyes traveled from my head down to my toes. "Where you been hiding?" he asked, staring at my breasts.

"Nowhere. I've been working," I said with an extra hint of attitude. I didn't want to divulge too much information in regards to my new work assignment with Parker. Plus, Jamel was out of control with his thirsty stares. I did not mind being eye candy, but Jamel was overeating.

"You wearin' that dress," he smiled, licking his lips.

"Don't talk too loud. Your girlfriend might hear," I said, nodding toward the entrance.

Elena walked in wearing a blue suit and black flats. The suit was fitted, but not too tight. Her hair was cut in layers and neatly curled. Looking closer, I noticed that she was wearing makeup. Despite my feelings toward her, I had to admit she actually looked nice.

"She's not my girlfriend," Jamel whispered.

"Good morning," Elena said happily. "How are you, Jamel?" she asked, staring at him affectionately.

"I'm fine," Jamel said coolly. "How are you?"

"Truly blessed," Elena replied. "How are you today, Asia?" she asked, looking at me.

I hesitated slightly before replying. "I'm good, Elena," I said slowly. "Thanks for asking."

There were several things that caught my attention.

One, Elena looked fifty times better than she usually did. Two, she called me by my first name and didn't cringe when I called her by hers. Three, she was glowing and smiling from ear to ear. I looked from Jamel to Elena and almost choked on my own tongue. I knew the glow and the goofy-ass look Elena had stamped across her face. It was the same one I had when I was sixteen years old and lost my virginity to Corey Jackson the night of my junior prom.

"Well, I should get going," she said, flashing Jamel a smile. "Have a good day, you two."

"You too," I said sweetly. Looking at Jamel, I crossed my arms across my chest.

"What?" he asked casually.

"You know what," I whispered. "You did it."

"Naw. I just spent a little time with her, that's all," he said, shrugging his shoulders. "Dinner."

It was obvious Jamel had me fucked up with the next broad. Looking at his attire, I looked back the entrance of the break room to the spot where I had noticed Elena's new suit. "Did she buy this shit?" I asked lowly, pointing from his head down to the gators on his feet.

His eyes shifted slightly to the left. "We went shopping together, but— "

"Did you hit it?" I asked impatiently.

"No!"

"You better hurry up and—"

"Why do you still have it out for her, Asia?" he asked.

"She ain't sweatin' you."

"She's not sweatin' me right now," I said, "but what happens when you drop her for the next man?"

"Besides, you can do all the pimpin' your ass wants after you handle my business." I snapped.

"As—" The sound of his cell phone beeping interrupted our conversation. He reached in his pocket and retrieved his Blackberry and looked at it.

"Is that her?" I asked, snatching the phone from his hands. A thumbnail of Elena's picture was on the left side of the screen, with text messages between the two of them on the right. From the text messages, I could see that Jamel was either playing his role right or he was actually digging Elena. I decided to cut the bullshit and get straight to the point.

"Yo, what you doing?" he asked, watching me as I composed a message.

Elena and I went back and forth several times until I finally came out and said what I thought Jamel should be thinking. I held my breath, waiting for Elena's reply. When his phone chimed, I smiled victoriously at the response. "Get a room this weekend," I said, handing him the phone.

Scanning the messages Jamel shook his head. "Yeah, alright," he said.

"Don't play with me, Jamel," I threatened. "I want proof. Video," I said firmly.

"You trippin'," he said. "I'm not going to record that shit."

"You don't have to," I said. "I'll be there to record it myself."

Jamel's eyes grew big. "Three way?"

"Hell no!" I said, disgusted. "You trippin'. She won't know I'm there."

"What are you going to do with the tape?" he asked.

"Keep it for collateral," I said. "That's all."

"Where will that leave me?" he asked. "She'll blame me," he whined, working my last nerve.

"I'm on the fifth floor working with Parker Bryant himself," I finally confessed. "You help me, and I'll make sure you get your own permanent spot at G&L."

"Adam is already putting a good word in for me," he said proudly.

"So what? Ol' boy got your back," I said. "The way things stand right now, there will be only one position filled."

"I got the CEO on my side," I whispered. "At the end of the day, which one of us do you think will land that position?"

Silence.

"Really," I said. "Think about it, boo boo."

*****

Parker was making it extra hard for me to get my flirt on by keeping me extra busy. Since returning with his coffee, he had me going nonstop with making phone calls, sending emails, and several other duties, including having his dry cleaning delivered. I reached out to his assistant,

Jessica, to get Parker's schedule for the rest of the week and to make sure she received the bouquet I had sent from Parker to wish her get well. Jessica was relieved when I told her I would handle her duties until she was well enough to return to the office. She immediately emailed me a long list of shit I knew a grown-ass man such as Parker was fully capable of doing himself and wished me luck. The experience caused me to develop a new respect for her and personal assistants everywhere. It was officially my opinion that being a personal assistant boiled down to doing everything but wiping your boss's ass and flipping out a titty to nurse them with.

By lunch I was starving and seriously craving a drink. The drink was out of the question, at least while I was on office duty, so I decided to settle for food to silence my grumbling stomach. After waiting for damn near forty minutes for Parker's lunch, I had to sign the credit card slip because Parker requested me to. Yes, you heard me right: the damn CEO doesn‘t even waste his time signing his own name! Anyway, after waiting forty minutes for the little man from the Chinese joint next door to deliver Parker's lunch, I was finally going to satisfy my own hunger.

Carrying the two large brown paper bags to Parker's office was a torture all its own. The aroma of the food had my stomach doing flip-flops. "Here's your lunch," I said, walking through his office door. I was so frustrated I didn't bother knocking. Setting the bags down on the desk, I gave him a faint smile. "Is there anything else I can get you?"

"One more thing," he said. "You don't have plans for lunch, do you?" he asked.

"No."

"Great, because I have a special assignment for you."

I watched as he rose from his desk and walked into his private bathroom, leaving me waiting for his next command. *What the hell?!* Inside, I could feel my anger rising. I am not a happy chick when I'm hungry. I could hear the water running in the bathroom, indicating Parker was using the office sink. *I know he ain't got me waiting while he washed his damn hands!* Crossing my arms across my breasts, I exhaled loudly. "I'm listening!" I said loudly. "What else?" I asked.

Parker reentered the room and slipped back behind the desk.

Want me to cut your food up in tiny little pieces? I thought. *Need a bib? Want me to burp your ass? What?* I was mentally ranting while physically waiting for Parker's response.

"Sit down," he instructed.

Doing as I was told, I plopped down in the chair facing him.

He was silent as he pulled the contents from the bags and set them on his desk one by one. Once he had all the containers open, he looked at me and smiled. "Lunch," he said. "I didn't know what you wanted, so I ordered a little bit of everything."

There are very few people in the world that surprise me, and Parker Bryant had officially become one of them.

"Wow," I sighed lightly, looking at the spread. "Thank you. I'm impressed."

"My little way of saying thanks for your hard work these last couple of days," he smiled.

His thanks would have been better if it came with keys to my own whip, but you have to crawl before you can walk. "Thank you," I said sincerely. "I'm pleasantly surprised."

"I normally don't surprise people," he said. "I usually always have a plan and make sure those involved are aware of it."

"What happens if your plan has to change?"

Digging into the container of teriyaki chicken, he answered, "That's why you always have a back-up plan."

"You can't plan for everything," I debated. "Spontaneity has often been better than anything I could have ever planned."

"Being spontaneous can get you in trouble," he spoke in between bites.

"Sometimes trouble can be good." I smiled slyly.

He looked at me, laughed slightly, and shook his head. "I try hard to avoid trouble," he said.

"I think it may be too late for that," I said softly but spoke loud enough for him to hear me.

Wiping the corners of his mouth with his napkin, he smiled and ordered, "Eat before your food gets cold."

*****

Parker and I were headed toward the elevator when my

cell phone rang.

"Hey, Trace," I answered. "I'm on my way out."

"Sorry, A," she said hurriedly from the other end of the phone. "I'm running late. I had an emergency at the office."

"No problem. I'll hang around here until you're done."

"Okay, sis. I'll see you as soon as I'm through."

"Be safe," I told her before hanging up.

"Problem?" Parker asked, looking over at me.

"No. My friend is just running a little behind," I explained, "so I'm going to hang out in the library until she picks me up."

"I'll wait with you," he said as we approached the elevator.

"Thanks, but I'll be fine," I told him as we stepped out the elevator. "I don't want to hold you up."

"I don't feel comfortable leaving you alone," he frowned. "Let me at least give you a ride home."

The thought of me relaxing while riding shotgun in a Ferrari was one I was definitely feeling, but I didn't want Parker to see the crummy neighborhood I lived in. "I can't let you do that," I said. "Besides, your schedule says you have an eight o'clock dinner party you can't miss."

We exited the elevator, stepping out into the empty lobby.

"Well, the sooner I get you home, the earlier I'll be able to get home and get ready for it," he said firmly. "Otherwise, we'll sit here together and wait on your friend. It's your choice," he added.

"Fine!" I exhaled loudly "You can take me home."

Inside Parker's car, I text Tracey to let her know she didn't have to pick me up and that I was gonna bum a ride with Parker. I could practically hear her screaming in her message as she replied, demanding a play-by-play when she called me later.

Parker's car still had that new car fresh leather smell. I wondered how long he had the whip but decided against asking him. The last thing I wanted him to think was that I was a gold-digger. Parker started the engine, and the sounds of Marsha Ambrosius' "Far Away" immediately flowed through the car stereo speakers.

"You're into Marsha?" he asked, looking over at me.

"I've been digging her since Floetry was together," I advised him. "I love her voice."

"I do too," he said. "It's sensual with just the right hint of funk."

"Exactly."

"What other kind of music do you like?"

"I like all types of music," I told him. "Just as long as it sounds good and I can move to it. What about you?" I asked.

"Hip hop, R&B, jazz—"

"Hip Hop?" I laughed, looking over at him.

"What's wrong with that?"

"Nothing. You just don't strike me as the type," I confessed. "I was thinking you were more along the lines of Bette Midler or Barry Manilow." I was teasing about Bette and Barry, but I was serious about my not taking him as the kind of man that got into hip hop.

"Funny," he chuckled.

"Seriously, name one hip hop artist you listen to."

"I listen to more than one."

"Well, one artist you have in your changer," I said, calling his bluff.

"Young Money."

"What do you know about Young Money?" I teased, turning in the seat to face him. "Name one artist from the Young Money clique."

"I can actually name them all," he said, navigating onto the interstate, "but since you only asked for one, Nikki Minaj."

"Besides what you've heard on the radio, what do you know about Nikki?"

"She's talented, business savvy, and sexy," he said. The way the word "sexy" rolled off his tongue made my nipples slightly hard.

"You know nothing about sexy," I teased.

"Just because I don't always acknowledge it doesn't mean I'm not aware that it's there." He looked over at me quickly before returning his focus and attention to the road ahead. There was something suggestive and sultry in his voice. Parker pulled up in front of my building and shifted the car into park. "I'll walk you to your door."

"No, I got it from here," I said, quickly unbuckling the seatbelt.

"This is not up for discussion," he said firmly.

"I know," I said, "so thank you and goodni—"

Before I could finish my sentence, he had the driver's side door open and closed and was making his way around the car to the passenger side. Holding the car door open, he watched as I stepped out of the car.

"Thank you," I whispered. The two of us stood face to face, staring into each other's eyes. Allowing my eyes to travel down to his lips, I licked mine lightly. The image of our lips locked and tongues pressing together entered my head, causing my pussy to tingle. Stepping back so he could close the door, I exhaled slowly. The two of us walked in silence to my front door. Once there, I waited for Parker to say "Goodbye, see you later, deuces" or anything, but he didn't. He just patiently waited as I fumbled with my keys and then finally opened my front door.

"Thank you again, "I said, opening the door and stepping backwards into my apartment.

"Maybe I should come in and make sure everything is safe inside," he said, looking over my head inside my apartment.

"Everything's fine," I said, smiling nervously. "Thank you for bringing me home." I was ready for him to leave. I know a lot of brothers are trying to prove that chivalry isn't dead, but damn, he was going above and beyond the call of duty.

"Are you sure you don't want me to check out the inside for you?" he asked. There was a hint of what I felt was concern in his voice.

"No, I'm fine," I said. "Thank you again."

"Have a good night, Asia," he smiled before turning and walking away.

I shut the door then exhaled. Looking around my living room, I scanned for my normal unwelcomed insect visitors, and sure enough, I saw a tiny roach scurrying across the floor. I was thankful Parker had not forced his way in, demanding to be my top-flight security for the night by checking for intruders.

I ran to the kitchen to retrieve my can of Raid. "If ya'll don't stop invading my space, Ima need you to start kicking in on the rent," I said, spraying the bug killer down on the insects. *Soon I will be up and out of this hellhole,* I thought to myself. I was saving a little from each paycheck to get myself a car, and then I would focus on a crib. The sooner I could focus on a new apartment, the better. I had managed to avoid Quick Rick since our encounter in Saks, but I didn't know how much longer he would go without putting me on blast throughout the entire neighborhood.

* * * * *

"Girl, you should have let his ass in!" Tracey screamed from the other end of the phone.

"For what? So he can see my unwelcomed tenants running across the floor?" I said, sucking my teeth. "No thank you!"

"You so crazy," she laughed. "Hell, at least he would have known how bad you need the job."

"All he has to do is ask, and I'll tell him how bad I need the job," I said, stretching out across my bed. Flashbacks of the two of us standing face to face outside his car ran through my head. *Hell, if he lets me, I'll show him*, I thought to myself.

"I'm thinking Mr. CEO may have some indecent intentions," Tracey said, smacking her lips.

"What do you mean?"

"How many CEOs you know who drive their employees home to the 'hood?" she asked. "Hell, G &L has security. You would have been perfectly fine waiting up in the building."

Tracey had a point. In addition to the security on the premises, there were other cars in the parking lot, so I would not have been alone. Still, I took Parker's generosity with a grain of salt, meaning I wasn't trying to read anything extra in to his offer to take me home or walk me in. The man was a gentleman. True, it was obvious he was attracted to me, but he still wasn't making any major moves.

"True, but I'm not your average employee," I giggled. "I'm a seductress. Men flock to my rescue."

"Say what you want, seductress," Tracey laughed. "Mr. CEO may have a couple tricks up his sleeves."

"He can bring them." I yawned, rolling onto my back. "I just hope he's prepared for mine."

Chapter 13

I sat in Parker's office, taking notes on a memo he wanted me to send out to each department.

He brought up the previous nights events. "I hope I didn't get you in trouble with your boyfriend last night," he said, looking across the desk at me.

"What? What boyfriend?"

"The one you live with," he stated. "That's why you didn't want me to come in, right?"

"I don't have a boyfriend," I said. "Remember? I told you I was single."

"Roommate?"

"Not even a dog," I said, taking a deep breath and then exhaling slowly. I knew the question was coming, asking me why I had acted so strangely at my door. I decided to beat him to the punch. "I just…just didn't want you to come in," I confessed.

"Oh, I see."

"It's nothing against you," I explained. "It's just that my place is a little sh…crappy."

"I knew the condition of the area when you gave me the

directions," he said. "Although it concerns me that you live in that area, it's nothing to be ashamed of."

"I'm just waiting for the day when I can do better," I said. "Much better."

"What about your family?"

"My father died when I was a baby, and my mother lives in Huntsville," I explained. "The two of us are not close. I have a grandmother who tries to help when she can, but she's on a fixed income."

"I have a feeling things are going to turn around for you soon," he said. "Speak it into existence."

"I have a feeling you're right," I said, "and thank you for your concern. It means a lot," I said honestly.

"Not a problem," he said. "Also, if there is anything I can do for you, let me know."

"Thank you. I will." I had a list of things I wanted to tell him, but I decided to let the cards fall on their own. "If that's all for now, I'm going to go get this typed up," I said, rising from my chair.

"Thank you, Asia."

I gave him a small smile before pulling the door shut. I hurried to the receptionist desk and flipped out my cell phone. I dialed Tracey's number, only to get her voicemail. "Hey, sis. Just wanted to let you know I have a ride home tonight," I said sweetly. "Talk to you later. Love ya!"

* * * * *

The workday seemed to rush by, and before Parker and

I knew it, it was quitting time.

"Thank you again for the ride," I said, looking over at him. "I completely forgot my friend had a staff meeting," I lied.

"It's no problem at all," he said. Relaxing in the passenger seat, I hummed along to R Kelly's "When a Woman Loves" playing on the radio. The sound of Parker's Blackberry ringing caused me to pause my humming.

"Hi," he said. "I'll be there in a half-hour. Love you too," he said, before pressing the end call button.

"Your lady?" I asked.

"Yes," he said lowly.

"Question."

"Yes?"

"Why haven't you married her?"

"Not the right time," he said. "We still have a lot to figure out."

"No offense, but if you haven't figured it out in five years..." I said, intentionally leaving him hanging.

"Breaking free isn't always the easiest thing to do," he said.

"For whom?" I asked. "You or her?"

"Both."

Parker pulled into my complex and shifted his car into park. "I'm walking you to the door," he said firmly, "and I'm not taking 'no' for an answer when I offer to escort you in."

"But—"

"No buts," he said, as he opened the passenger door.

Parker and I walked in silence until we reached my door. I wondered how many unwanted guests were waiting on me this time. My heart skipped a beat nervously when I saw that my front door had been kicked in.

"Wait here!" Parker ordered.

After Parker made sure that the culprits were gone, we stood inside my living room surveying the damage. The place looked like an F-2 tornado had swallowed it and thrown it back up. My furniture was turned over, and there was glass everywhere from my broken coffee tables. My thirty-two-inch TV was gone. My bedroom had also been ransacked; the mattress and box spring were flipped over, and my underwear were all over the floor. I quickly went to the drawer where I kept my grandmother's ring. I had only recently gotten it back from the pawn shop, and I would have died on the spot if it was gone. To my relief, it was still tucked in the sock I kept it in, along with the few hundred dollars I had hidden. Looking at my closet, I saw my wardrobe was intact with the exception of my Dior dress. The only evidence left of my dress was the hanger it had been hanging on. *Son of a bitch!* I cursed to myself while tears trickled down my face.

"Probably some addict looking for money or something to pawn," Parker said soothingly. "They've probably been watching you come and go. Did you have renter's insurance?" he asked.

"No," I sniffled. "When it freakin' rains it freakin' pours."

Putting his arm around me, Parker held me tightly.

"Everything happens for a reason," he said, "and everything is going to be alright. I promise."

I snuggled into his arms while crying softly.

*****

Slipping the plush bathrobe over my shoulders, I secured the belt tightly around my waist. After checking into the executive suite at the Ritz-Carlton, I decided to take a hot bubble bath to ease my muscles and relax my mind. After we replaced my door, Parker insisted that I check into a hotel. "You never know if or when they might return," he said. "My conscious won't allow me to leave you here. We have a corporate account at the Ritz," he explained on the drive to the hotel. "The staff is exceptional, and anything you want can be charged to the room."

I was still depressed and in tears at that moment but grateful at the same time. "Thank you," I cried.

When we arrived, Parker ensured that I had no problems checking in but denied me the pleasure of his coming up to the room with me. "I have to get home," he said. "She's waiting."

There was a look of guilt and regret on his face, and I wondered if it was for me or for her. I told him I understood and kissed his cheek softly.

It was a shame that Parker had declined, but it was a sheer delight to be away from the 'hood, if only for one night. I poured myself another glass of Moscato and climbed into the king-sized bed. I contemplated calling my bestie, but looking at the clock I saw it was just after eleven p.m. Tracey normally turned her phone off by ten thirty, and the chances of me actually speaking to her were slim to none, but I decided to call her anyway and leave a message. Sipping slowly, I picked up the hotel phone and dialed Tracey's number.

"This is Tracey," she answered on the third ring.

"What you doing up, sis?"

"Going over some listings," she said, blowing into phone. "Bullshit. I'm just trying to stay focused."

"What's wrong?"

"I want you to know my hubby has yet to make it in from his meeting," she said, anger bubbling in her voice.

"Did you talk to him?"

"Yeah, over an hour ago," she said. "Asia, he is full of shit! That muthafucka ain't showing houses at this time of night!"

I wanted to agree with her, but at the same time, I wanted to hold on to a glimmer of hope that Harold was actually handling business and that the business was not another woman.

"You know how clients can be," I said lightly. "I'm sure he's not doing anything wrong."

"We will see," she said. "And whose number are you calling from?" she asked.

"The Ritz," I smiled.

"The Ritz who?"

"Ritz Carlton crazy."

"What the hell you doing at the Ritz Carlton?" she yelled.

"Chillin' in the executive suite," I bragged, "sippin' on Moscato."

"How did you get there?" she questioned. "And why didn't you invite me?"

"Parker put me up for the night," I said.

"What?!" she chanted. "Wait…is he there with you?" she whispered into the phone. "Did ya'll fu—"

"No and no," I answered, cutting her off. "Hush and listen."

After filling her in on what had taken place that night and giving her some details of the tension and contact between Parker and myself, I sighed.

"I thought I was your best friend," she said, sounding insulted.

"You are."

"Then why am I just now finding out that you and Mr. CEO have a thang going on?"

"We don't have a thang going on, and—"

"You don't my ass!" she screamed, cutting me off again. "Damn near making out in the office, suites at the Ritz. It's about to go down!"

There was a knock at the door.

"Hold on," I said, laying the phone on the bed. I could still her Tracey talking on the other end of the receiver as I ran through the open French doors into the living room. Standing on my tiptoes, I peeked out the peephole. Running back to the phone, I quickly retrieved the receiver. "Let me call you back," I whispered.

"What?" she asked. "Why? Is that him? That's him, isn't it? I told you!" she said. "He want that. It's damn near midnight, and he—"

"I'll call you back," I whispered.

"Love you. Bye." I hung up on her before she had the chance to finish her sentence. There was a light knock again.

Opening the door, I smiled at Parker, standing with his hands neatly folded in front of him. He wore a red button-down shirt and black slacks. The jacket he wore earlier, along with the tie, were both gone.

"I didn't order any room service," I teased, stepping back to let him in.

"Am I interrupting?" he asked, staring at the robe.

"Not at all," I said, "but shouldn't you be at home?" I asked.

"We had an argument," he said, walking over and sitting down on the edge of the sofa. "I wasn't in the mood for the screaming tonight."

"She's mad because you were late?" I concluded, shutting the door and securing the lock.

"Again," he said. "I remember there was a time when she understood and loved my dedication to the company and my staff."

"Some things get old," I said, walking over and sitting down next to him. "Besides, you have to make sure home is taken care of first."

"It's not just the business," he said, rubbing his hands together. "She's changed. I've changed."

"How?"

"She's jealous," he continued. "And I'm reckless."

"Reckless?" I asked, looking over at him. "Explain."

"Doing too many things I know I shouldn't," he said. "I know better."

Silence

"But when I left, there was only one thing on my mind," he said.

"What's that?"

"Coming here and seeing you."

I remained silent as I watched him walk from the sofa to the entrance of the bedroom. He leaned against the doorframe, standing with his hands in his pockets. He had made the first move, and I felt it was time for me to handle the rest. I looked at him in silence. His eyes were clear and wide, and they told me he was ready. I walked across the room and extended my hand to him. I had never realized until I was standing barefoot looking up at him how much taller he was than me when I wasn't wearing heels. I loved it.

Leaning down, Parker kissed me slowly and softly. His tongue was warm and inviting as it found mine, and together the two of them created their own rhythm. His lips felt better than I could have ever imagined. They were smooth and soft, and I wanted more of them. Sucking on his bottom lip gently, I slowly began to unbutton his shirt. Pushing the material off his shoulders onto the floor, I admired Parker's body. He had nice, well-defined biceps, a chiseled chest, and a six-pack. The patch of hair in between his pecks was straight and fine, similar to that on top of his head. Stepping back, I led him by the hand over to the bed. Climbing onto the bed backwards, I slowly untied the robe, allowing it to fall open. Parker watched me intently as I slipped my arms out of the garment and then tossed it onto the floor. When I saw the corners of his lips turn up into a small smile, I knew he was pleased with what he saw. Slowly stepping out of his pants and then his boxers, he kept his eyes locked with mine. When he was completely undressed, he stood by the bed, naked and fine. Parker had the perfect package from his head right down to his toes. His dick was hard and far above average. It was perfect.

Climbing on top of me, he kissed my lips and then slowly moved down to my breasts. Parker sucked my left nipple gently while massaging my right one in between his thumb and index finger. He alternated between the two of them until they were so hard they hurt. Parker planted kisses from my breasts down to my belly button until he reached my clean-shaven kitten. He held my lips open with his hands as his tongue searched and explored the wetness he had created. Grabbing his head with both hands, I rotated my hips, grinding against his warm mouth until his lips were drenched with my sweet juices. He positioned his body between my legs and then stopped. "One second," he said.

I watched as he removed a pack of condoms from his pants pockets. *Thank you!* I thought to myself. I was thankful that he was not only fine and rich, but smart as well.

After retrieving the condom, he secured our protection on his hardness before repositioning himself between my legs. He took his time entering me, slowly feeding inch by inch of his dick to my pussy. As we kissed, he made strong, calculated rotations, hitting every crevice of my walls and building heated pleasure on my hot spot. I could feel my body perspiring from inside, another orgasm pushing toward the surface. Sucking on his earlobe, I moaned, not recognizing my own voice. Wrapping my legs around him I held his dick tightly with my inner muscles, as I rotated my hips and matched his rhythm. My orgasms came hard, one followed by another. Parker pushed my legs forward until my knees were pressed against my breasts. The room echoed with the sound of his sac slapping my sweat-drenched ass and the gushing of my watery kitten. His breathing became heavy and rugged as he pounded and drilled deep inside my wet hole.

"Shit..." I moaned, as my legs began to tremble. Wrapping my ankles around his neck, I pulled him closer.

Together with our bodies entwined, skin pressed against skin, we fucked until I felt his muscles getting tense and heard him moan as he said my name. "Asia..."

*****

Milk does your body good, but a good nut does it better. I am living proof. I was satisfied and exhausted after Parker's and my sex session. After taking a shower together, the two of us ordered breakfast and then stretched across the bed. Parker was extremely quiet, and curiosity had me wondering what was going on inside his head.

"Regrets?" I asked, running my fingers across his chest.

"I don't believe in regrets," he said, stroking my bare back. "I believe in consequences but never regrets."

"What do you mean?" I asked, propping myself up to look at him.

"I've crossed the line one too many times," he said.

"Do you want to go back to before?" I asked. "My relentless flirting and your constant refusal?"

"It's too late for that," he laughed, "but I do like the subtle side of you."

"Subtle is boring," I said, rolling my eyes.

"There is nothing boring about you Asia," he said, stroking my face. "Mysterious maybe, but far from boring."

Climbing on top of him, I straddled his waist. "Being mysterious is a good thing," I said, kissing him softly on the lips. "Right?" I asked.

"It can be," he said, massaging my naked breast. "But it can also be dangerous."

Sliding down his body, I stopped in between his legs. Taking his partially hard dick in my hand, I licked, then sucked the head slowly.

"Mmm," he moaned, grabbing my hair.

Rolling my tongue across his dick, I massaged his sac gently. "Have you ever known danger to feel this good?" I asked.

"No…no," he groaned, "but then I do try to avoid it."

"Mission failed," I said, before opening my mouth wide and taking all of him in.

I deep throated Parker's dick hungrily. I could feel his body getting tense as I alternated between sucking just the head then deep-throated him again and again.

"Ohhhhh," Parker moaned.

Locking my jaws I bobbed up and down on his rock hard man until his pre-cum seeped onto my tongue. The small shot of Parker's juices tasted sweet to me and evoked my curiosity. I wanted to taste more of him. I began to suck harder, impatiently waiting for Parker to release his men in the back of my throat. Parker thrust his hips upward while holding my head in place. Opening my lips I allowed him to fuck my mouth until his dick was dripping with my saliva.

"Here it comes," he grunted. " Here it comes!" Pushing his hands down, I held his wrist at his sides, penned against the bed.

"Fuck…" Parker blurted, as he came, pumping his warm-sweet cum in my mouth. I held my lips tightly around him, capturing every drop of his fluid. Looking up, I stared into Parker's eyes. A look of shear pleasure was etched out in his face. I swallowed hard before sucking him off again.

* * * * *

After putting Parker to sleep, I slipped on jeans and a t-shirt and then went downstairs. DeAngelo stood by the entrance of the hotel waiting for me. DeAngelo lived in my complex. The two of us had kicked it a couple of times but never hooked up. DeAngelo was a bona fide hustler but a gentleman at the same time.

"Yo, you on some more shit, shawty," De Angelo stated, looking around the hotel lobby. "Big shit."

"I'm trying," I said, reaching into my jeans pocket.

"That's what's up," he said, nodding his head.

I watched as a tall, light-skinned female with bright red highlights throughout her hair walked through the hotel entrance and entered the lobby. The woman's face needed some work, but her body was banging in the fitted above-the-knee designer dress she wore. "Baby, I'm ready to go," she whined, kissing DeAngelo's cheek. "Hello," she said, smiling at me.

"Hello," I sung, mimicking the woman. "Nice dress," I said bitterly.

"Thank you!" she chanted, spinning around. "Delo bought it for me. It's a Dior," she said, over enunciating the word.

"Yes," I said sarcastically. "I know."

"Stop showcasing," DeAngelo said firmly. "Go wait in the car. I'll be out in a minute."

Pouting, the woman marched off like a three-year-old who had just been reprimanded by her father. Flashing me a smile, he laughed lightly.

"Here you go," I said, sucking my teeth. I handed him a crisp one-hundred-dollar bill.

"I thought you said two bills, ma," he said. stuffing the money in his pocket.

"I did," I said sarcastically. "That was before you gave your little gutter rat my dress!"

"You told me to make the shit look real," he said, throwing his hands up. "Who you know would leave that shit behind?"

"And my TV?" I asked, crossing my arms across my chest.

"Hell, sometimes you got to give to get," he said. "Looking at this joint, what you gave ain't half as much as what you getting in return."

He had a point, so I decided to give him the other hundred. He had done what I asked him to do and then some. Plus, I never knew when I might need him on my team.

Chapter 14

"My last tenant ended up purchasing her own house," Parker explained to me.

It was a beautiful Friday afternoon, and the two of us had played hooky from work. After leaving the office, he took me to view one of three properties he owned in Georgia. He looked at me affectionately as the two of us stood in the living room of his 3600-plus-square-foot brownstone. "The property is only a year old, and I personally guarantee everything is in excellent working condition."

The brownstone included four bedrooms and four and a half baths. The master suite came with a fireplace, a private covered terrace, a master bath with a morning bar, a whirlpool tub, and separate standing shower. In addition to having a large rooftop deck, the brownstone came with a three-car garage, huge storage room, and a wine room. To state that I had been upgraded would have been an understatement and an insult. The brownstone was breathtaking.

"You can decorate and make any changes you like," Parker said, handing me the keys.

"Thank you, but the rent here has to be at least a couple grand," I said, shaking my head. "I can't afford this."

"It's actually four grand plus," he said matter-of-factly.

What the hell? I thought to myself. I knew the gated community of Habersham where the brownstone was located looked pricey, but four grand was a lot. Frowning, I withdrew my hand and refused to accept the keys. "I can't," I said.

"I never asked you for rent or anything else," he said. "You can stay here as long as you like, no questions asked, no strings attached." The look in his eyes told me he was being sincere.

Taking the keys, I smiled excitedly. "I promise to pay you back when I can," I said. "After I get a promotion," I added, dropping a subtle hint.

"You have a deal."

Grabbing his hand, I pulled him to me and then down to the hardwood floor. Straddling his waist, I kissed his lips gently, parting them with my tongue. I could feel his nature rising underneath me, and I loved the way his body reacted to my simple touch.

"I do want something from you," he breathed, turning his head as I slowly licked and then sucked his neck.

"What's that?"

"Promise me you will never betray my trust," he said.

"Okay," I answered, unbuttoning his pants.

Grabbing me by the hair, Parker gently pulled my head back. Staring at me intently, he searched my eyes with his.

"Promise me," he ordered. The darkness in his eyes sent goose bumps across my skin.

"I promise," I said.

Stroking my face with his fingertips, he said softly, "I can give you anything you want—things you never imagined—but never betray me. I told you, I don't believe in regrets, but I do believe in consequences." His words were spoken gently, but something told me there was a hidden threat lying in the fiber of their meaning.

"I understand," I said.

He seemed to relax as he rolled on top of me while spreading my legs with his body.

"Welcome home, Asia," he smiled before kissing me hard on the mouth.

I reciprocated while his words replayed in my head.

Parker's kiss became more intense with every stroke of our tongues. Slipping his hands underneath my skirt, Parker pushed my panties to the side then slipped his index finger into my pussy. Instantly all thoughts of our conversation dissipated and my body began responding to his touch.

"Damn," I groaned, as Parker slipped one finger in and out of my pussy while massaging the hood of my protruding clit with the other. Parker flicked his tongue across my clit, once then twice before taking it in his mouth. He nibbled on my clit gently while plunging his finger deeper inside of me. My heart rate increased rapidly as Parker began to suck my clit like a baby nursing on its mother's tit.

"Cum for me," he ordered. Grabbing his head I pushed

his face further into my pussy. I could feel my self on the brink of a sexual explosion. Guiding my hand to my clit, Parker watched me closely. Stroking my clit rapidly I stared down at him. The look in his eyes told me he was ready and anticipating what I was preparing to give him. The thought of him sipping my cum made me even hotter. I arched my back as my pussy rained, splashing him in his handsome face.

"Shiiit!" I screamed. Parker rolled his tongue back and forth across his saturated lips while unbuttoning his pants. Before I could blink or relax from my climax, he had his dick out and was diving into my pussy.

Chapter 15

I had forgotten about the appointment I had set with Jamel earlier in the week. In fact, I had forgotten all about Elena and G&L altogether. I was too caught up enjoying the benefits and privileges Parker was bestowing upon me. After treating me to a shopping spree that included furniture and grocery shopping Friday night, he made me a candlelit dinner which the two of us enjoyed on the rooftop of the brownstone. We had turned off our phones per his request and dedicated the time we shared to each other. I didn't mind. Parker knew how to hold my attention, and at that moment he was doing and giving me exactly what I wanted. I was in my own world, and it felt good.

The next morning, I woke to find Parker gone and a note, a thousand dollars, and his credit card lying on the night stand. I smiled as I read his letter.

Good morning, beautiful,

I truly enjoyed last night. Sorry I sneaked out, but I didn't want to wake you. I have business to take care of today, but I will call you when I get the chance. Treat yourself today and buy whatever you need. There is a car and driver downstairs waiting for you. Enjoy.

P.B.

Running to the window excitedly, I pulled back the drapes. Sure enough, there was a black and silver Maybach parked outside. "I can get use this," I said, snatching my cell phone off the marble nightstand. I turned on my phone, and my message indicator immediately started beeping. Checking my voicemail, I discovered I had ten messages. One was from my mother, and the rest were all from Tracey.

"Hello?" Tracey sounded like she had been beaten down on the other end of the phone.

"Hey, boo!" I chimed.

"Where you been?" she asked, clearing her throat. "I called you all night," she said.

"I'm sorry," I said sincerely. "Are you alright?" I asked.

"I am now." She exhaled. There was obvious tension and frustration in her voice.

"Get up and get dressed," I said. I was concerned about the obvious trouble in my best friend's voice, but at the same time I was still excited to share my own news.

"What for?"

"You're goin' shopping with me," I said smiling. "We can talk about last night and have lunch wherever you want."

"I'm not in the mood for shopping," she said, sounding depressed, "but you can buy me a drink."

Looking at the clock, I observed that it was only nine a.m. "Trace, what's wrong?" I asked, sitting down on the edge of the bed.

"Harold," she said. "That muthafucka's been playing me."

After listening to a brief rundown of what has transpired between the two of them, I finally said, "Get dressed. I'm on my way."

"How you getting here?" she asked.

"Just get up," I said, smiling. "I'm on my way."

* * * * *

Tracey opened the door wearing a fitted Ed Hardy t-shirt and white leggings. Her hair, which was normally perfect without a strand out of place, was pulled back in a low ponytail. Her eyes were red and puffy, letting me know she had been crying for hours before. She looked completely worn out and defeated.

I gave her a big hug and then stepped through the doorway into her living room. "Damn!" I stated, looking around the room. There were broken lamps and piles of what I assumed to be Harold's clothes cut and torn scattered across the floor.

Walking over to her sofa, Tracey plopped down next to an empty bottle of Jack Daniel's.

"I told you his ass was up to something," she said,

smoothing her hands over her hair. "When he started trippin' about money and nit-picking every little thing," she said, "it was a damn sign."

Tracey had explained over the phone that she had gone through Harold's phone while he was sleeping and found text messages and X-rated pictures from one of his business associates. She said when she confronted him about what she had found, he confessed that he had been sleeping with the woman for the past month.

"Where is he now?" I asked, sitting down beside her.

"At a hotel," she said, shrugging her shoulders. "At least that's what came up on the caller ID when he called for the one hundredth time today. I called the bitch," she said, laughing lightly. "That ho had the nerve to tell me she loves my husband and she ain't goin' nowhere."

"What did you tell her?"

"I asked her if he was worth dying over," she said smugly.

I looked at Tracey and waited for her to say something or laugh, but she didn't.

"She told me yes, A," Tracey said, shaking her head. "I told her to be careful," she added.

"It doesn't matter what she said," I told her. "Harold loves you. He was wrong for what he did, but he loves you. Christina was a fling—nothing more and nothing less."

"Maybe, "she mumbled, looking at me. "Wait...how did you know it was Chrissy?" she asked.

I had put my foot in my mouth and choked myself. I

decided to tell Tracey what I had witnessed the day of the party.

"Why didn't you tell me?" she asked, raising her voice.

"I didn't know how," I said, watching her pace back and forth, "and I knew eventually if it was something, it would come out."

"You should have told me," she said angrily. "You're supposed to be my fucking friend! A real friend would have told me."

"What you mean by *supposed to be* and a *real* friend?" I asked with slight attitude. "I am your friend, and I've always been real with you."

"Whatever," she said, rolling her eyes.

I could understand why Tracey was upset with me, but I also wanted her to understand why I kept the incident with Harold and Christina a secret. "My telling you wouldn't have changed a thing," I said.

"I would have known who to fucking watch," she snapped, standing with her hands on her hips. "She wouldn't have been all up in my house playing nice with me."

"I'm sorry I didn't tell you, Trace, but I stand by my decision."

"And I stand by this one," she said, walking over and opening the door. "Get out."

I was shocked but hurt even more from her behavior toward me. As I left her home with my head held high, I suppressed the tears struggling to get to the surface.

*****

I was determined to make the best out of my Saturday and take advantage of the courtesy shopping spree Parker was providing me. However, it would have been three times better having Tracey with me. I told myself she was the one being an asshole about the situation and that she would eventually come around.

After treating myself to the complete spa treatment, including a facial, massage, French manicure, and pedicure, I decided to do some shopping. After hitting the Louis Vuitton store up, I decided to raid the racks at Saks.

"Long time no see."

I recognized the sound of Quick Rick's voice before I turned around. *Not long enough*, I thought to myself.

"Oh you back on that boojie shit?" Quick Rick asked, watching me.

"Never got off it," I said, crossing my arms across my chest.

Licking his lips, Rick shook his head. "That's what I'm talking 'bout," he said. "A muthafucker try to be cool wit you, and you rather piss on him then speak."

"I don't believe in wasting my time on those I feel unworthy," I said casually.

"You did when this dick was in yo' mouth," he laughed, grabbing his crotch.

Rolling my eyes, I turned my back to him and continued to look through the rack of suits.

"You looking for something in particular?"

"What, you work here now?" I asked sarcastically. "You all legit now?"

"Naw, but I might be able to help you with what you need."

"Help yourself," I mumbled.

"Oh, so now you too good for my help?" he said, nodding his head. "Yeah, I got you."

"Answer this," he said. "You know why I wouldn't fuck you that day?" he asked, cocking his head to the side.

"Scared you couldn't keep up," I said, referring to the mediocre size of his penis.

"Naw," he chuckled, rubbing his hands together. "I wanted that ass to bow down—to show you how it felt to have a nigga like me look down on a fake-ass bitch like you."

I could feel my anger boiling inside me. Ignoring him, I continued to browse through the clothes.

"I musta seen you twenty to a hundred times in the 'hood," he continued. "Walking 'round wit your nose up in the air. For what? Cause your home girl got a nice whip? Cause you graduated? Ho you still ain't got shit," he said.

"And you ain't shit," I snapped lowly. "You never will be. You should feel honored that I would even allow you to get close to me."

"Honored? For what?" he taunted. "You just another ho in pretty packaging. You decorate the outside nicely, but the inside is still the same. A ho." Quick Rick turned and walked off, leaving me alone.

* * * * *

I stood at the cash register listening to the tall brunette verifying with the credit card company that Parker had granted me permission to use his card. I was frustrated and slightly annoyed that the process was taking close to thirty minutes. After my run-in with Quick Rick, I wanted to get as far away from that place as possible. To my dismay, he was still in the store moving from rack to rack casually, flashing me the occasional smile. I had noticed him a time or two concealing a dress in the bags he was carrying, and I wondered just how many dresses he had lifted in the time I had been standing at the counter.

"Thank you for your patience, Miss Turner," the cashier said, hanging up the phone. "Everything is fine, and you will not have this problem next time you shop with us."

"Thanks," I said, grabbing the bags from the counter.

"Is there anything else I can help you with?" she asked nicely.

My first thought was to tell her "no," but then I remembered there was one more thing I wanted. "Actually," I said lowly, "yes there is."

* * * * *

After my driver loaded my bags in the car, I asked him to wait before pulling away from the front of the store. I wanted to see Quick Rick one more time. Hell, who knew when I would see him again? Ten minutes later, I watched as he was escorted through the front doors in handcuffs to an awaiting patrol car. Smiling to myself, I blew a kiss out the window. I felt pure gratification at seeing Rick being hauled off in the back of the car. Earlier, when the brunette behind the counter asked me if I needed additional help, I politely informed her that the gentlemen in blue by the Dolce & Gabbana dresses had offered to sell me a stolen gown at half-price. The gentleman in blue was Rick. *Payback is so very sweet.*

"I'm ready," I said to the driver.

"Where to, Miss Turner?" he asked.

"Home." I laughed. "Home."

Chapter 16

The weekend was over, and we were back to business, but that did not stop Parker from bestowing gifts upon me. The diamond tennis bracelet shining on my wrist was evidence of that.

"Do you like it?"

"I love it." I smiled, throwing my arms around his neck. "Let me show you how much," I whispered in his ear.

Pulling back, he looked at me and smiled. "Just how do you plan to do that?"

"Sit down," I ordered. I waited until Parker was sitting in his office chair before walking around and easing down on my knees. Unbuckling his pants, I looked up at him and smiled. Parker had treated me all weekend long, from shopping to putting a little money in my bank account, to sexing me royally. I felt it was only right that I return the favor. Pulling his dick out, I slowly began to give him a hand job.

"That feels good," he whispered, running his fingers through my hair.

"I bet this feels better," I whispered, as I flicked my

tongue across his head.

"Yes."

"And this?" Taking the head of his hardness in my mouth, I sucked gently while rolling my tongue back and forth.

"Yesss" he groaned, looking down at me.

I winked my eye at him before I opened my mouth wide and deep-throated his dick. I was down on my knees giving Parker the straight business when there was a knock on his office door.

Parker jumped slightly, grabbing a handful of my hair. "Just a moment!" he yelled. The two of us sprung into action. He moved quickly to put his man up and fix his pants, and I hurried around to the other side of the desk. I smoothed my hands over my hair in the event that there was a hair out of place, and then I smiled innocently.

"It's open," Parker announced.

The door opened, and Nathaniel strolled in carrying a large hanging folder. "Good morning," he spoke to Parker. Looking over at me, he smiled. "How are you, Asia?" he asked.

"I'm fine, Nathaniel," I said sweetly. "How are you?"

"I'm good."

"What can I do for you, Nate?" Parker asked. He looked from Nate to me then back to Nate again. The tension in the room was thick enough to choke on.

"I wanted to drop off a copy of the proposal I was telling you about and to check on Asia and make sure everything is going smoothly," he said. Nathaniel's eyes lit up every time they fell on me. It was cute to me, but Parker's expression was one of disapproval and secretly spoke that he was annoyed with Nathaniel's presence.

"I'm fine," I said pleasantly. "Thank you."

"Don't worry, Nate," Parker said. "She's being well taken care of." There was an air of authority in Parker's voice.

"Just doing my job," Nathaniel said.

"Thanks, Nathaniel," Parker said, "and I'll be sure to check out your proposal."

"Great." Nathaniel smiled. "I think you'll find that this is the one to take G&L to the next level...and me to the next position," he added smoothly.

"We'll see," Parker said. "Thanks again."

"Thanks, Nate." I smiled.

"Anytime, Asia." He nodded at Parker before walking out, shutting the door behind him.

Parker waited for Nathaniel's departure before questioning me about our relationship.

"How well do you know Nate?" he asked, reclining in his chair.

"I only know what we learned in class."

Silence.

"I'm sure I'll find out lots more once I'm hired permanently," I said casually.

Parker looked away quickly but not fast enough to keep me from seeing the frown that stretched across his lips.

"What's wrong?" I asked, studying his expression.

"How would you like to continue working directly for me?"

"What do you mean?"

"What if I transfer Jessica to another department?" he suggested. "I'll keep you on as my permanent assistant."

The offer was tempting, but not that tempting. I hadn't endured four years of college to be his personal assistant, and I hadn't come to G&L to settle for taking Parker's notes and dictations. I wanted more, and I was determined to get it. "That's sweet, but no," I said. "I want to be more than just a secretary."

"You *are* more." He sounded offended, even on the verge of being angry. "I can make sure you are well compensated and that you want for nothing."

"Come here," I ordered, motioning with my finger for him to come closer. I waited until he was standing in front of me, leaning easily against the desk. I stood and wrapped my arms around his neck. I licked across the rim of his bottom lip and then kissed him softly. "You are too sweet, baby," I said seductively. I wanted to diffuse his anger and dissipate the tension that had been all too present since Nathaniel had entered the room. "But a woman always needs to have her own. I mean I've already broken my rule by moving into your brownstone," I added. It was true. I had given Parker power over me, in a sense. If he wanted to, he could dump my ass out on the street at any minute.

"If you want the brownstone, it's yours," he whispered,

pulling me closer.

"What?" I asked, baffled. "Really?"

"Yes really," he said. "There's property all over Atlanta. I can buy a new one at the blink of an eye if I want."

The thought of Parker just handing over the title had my mind reeling. Shaking the thought off, I returned to the discussion the two of us were having. "Well, it's not just that," I said gently. "I want my own office, and I want to see my name on the door. I don't want to just be Parker Bryant's assistant," I said. "I want to be a G&L superstar."

"You are a superstar," he said, pulling me closer.

"To you maybe," I sighed, "but I want the world to know."

Looking at me, Parker stroked my hair softly. "Is the career and title that important?" he asked.

"Yes."

"You're making this harder than it needs to be," he said, shaking his head.

Reaching down in front of me, I rubbed and massaged his crotch gently. His eyes narrowed to small pleasure-induced slits. "What?" I asked sensually. "This?"

"That too," he moaned.

Turning around, I rotated my hips, allowing my ass to grind against him. I could feel his dick getting harder and harder with every movement. Parker gently pushed me forward with one hand as he moved underneath my skirt with the other. Spreading my legs shoulder width apart, I moaned as he pulled my panties down to my knees and slowly inserted his finger inside of me.

Reaching behind me, I stroked his crotch harder. I felt a surge of excitement as he slowly began to stroke the crack of my ass.

Parker pushed my skirt up around my waist and then bent me forward. Grabbing the arms of the chair, I arched my back. Parker pushed his finger deep inside my pussy while rolling his tongue across my ample ass. My clit grew hard with anticipation, throbbing until I could no longer resist reaching down and rubbing it. Parker eased down to the floor and knelt behind me. He spread my ass cheeks open and then traced his tongue around the rim of my tightest hole. My knees went weak instantly when he pushed his wet tongue in and then out, in and then out of my asshole.

"Oh!" I moaned, bouncing back against his face. My kitty was soaking wet and ready. I heard his pants unzip then felt his rock hard manhood as he rubbed it back and forth across my ass. He was teasing me, pushing me to the point of no return. In between my legs it felt like I was on fire. I wanted to cum—I *needed* to cum. "Fuck me," I whispered.

Parker slid in me from behind. Grabbing my waist, he thrust forward fiercely, pumping in and out of my wet pussy. Parker spread the cheeks of my ass gently. I could hear him sucking on his finger as he continued to beat my kitty down from behind. When his finger pushed into my tight asshole, I felt like I would explode on impact.

“That feels good,” I moaned., grabbing my breast. Squeezing them gently I waited anxiously for what I knew was coming next.

Parker pulled his dick from my soaking wet pussy then slowly began to ease his dick in, replacing his finger. I had never had my hole penetrated but I was hot, wet, and ready for whatever. Parker took his time opening me. There was a brief moment of pain that was quickly overshadowed by pleasure. Parker rubbed my clit methodically, quickening as each inch of his dick slid inside me. I was completely turned on. When Parker began pushing his dick in and out, fucking me in my ass, I knew I was only inches away from being completely turned out. Looking back over my shoulder, I bounced, causing my cheeks to jiggle wildly.

Clenching the arms of the chair tightly, I backed up some more. I met his beats pound for pound. Grabbing me by my hair, he groaned as I bounced hard on his dick. Biting down on my bottom lip, I came hard but quietly. Parker continued to thrust deeply until finally pulling out of my hole and shooting his warm cum all over my ass.

*****

After lunch, I was still high from the dick-down Parker had given me earlier and still reflecting upon the wonderful weekend I had. Parker seemed happy and stress free, and together we were working like a well-oiled machine. However, our locomotive was about to come to a screeching halt.

The two of us had just returned from a meeting with the marketing team when we walked into his office and found Jessica sitting behind what I had been affectionately referring to as *my* desk. She sat going over paperwork as we walked through the door. Jessica was a cute long-haired brunette with blue eyes the color of ocean waves and a small frame. Parker had told me she was in her early thirties, but looking at her, you would have thought she was easily approaching forty. "Good morning," she said with a smile, looking at Parker and then at me.

"Jessica," Parker said, his eyebrows raised. "You're back."

"I am," she chimed sweetly, looking at me. "Just can't stay away."

"Jessica, this is Asia," Parker said. "Asia, this is Jessica."

"Hello," I said, faking a smile.

"It's nice to finally meet you, Asia," she said, standing. "I've heard great things about you."

"Thank you," I said. I was not feeling the fact that Jessica had returned her happy ass back to work and was about to send mine bouncing back downstairs with Nathaniel and Jamel.

"That is a gorgeous tennis bracelet," she said staring at my wrist.

"Thank you," I said politely. "It was a gift."

"Cartier?" she said, turning up her lips. "You must be something special to receive such an extravagant gift."

"I am someone special," I informed her, "and the person

who gave it to me is someone special to me."

"I'm sure," she said.

"What are you working on?" Parker asked, looking at the documents lying on the desk.

"I'm just playing catch-up to see where we stand," she said. "Making sure everything is in its proper place."

"Asia has been doing an excellent job." Parker smiled, looking over at me. "She has left no stone unturned while filling in for you."

"I do what I can," I said sweetly.

"Well, now that Mr. Bryant's assistant is back, you can continue your internship," Jessica said loudly. "Thank you for filling in, but I'm here, and I'm back on my job."

From my previous phone conversations with the woman, I thought she and I might have ended up being cool, but now that she was back at the office, it was obvious that she felt I was invading her territory. I also felt like she was invading mine.

"That said," she continued, "it was nice meeting you, and I'll see you soon."

I cut my eyes at Parker to let him know I didn't like the way his pencil pusher was coming at me. "That you will. Parker, I'll see you later," I said, turning on my heels to leave.

"Asia, before you go," he said quickly, "may I speak to you in my office?"

Nodding my head, I stormed toward his office door.

"Would you like me to come take dictation?" Jessica

asked.

"That won't be necessary," Parker said, following behind me and shutting the door. "Asia, my offer still stands," he said once we were alone. "I'll transfer her to another department."

"My feelings haven't changed about that," I said with attitude. "I just wasn't expecting her back so soon."

"I know. Neither was I," he said. "I've enjoyed every moment with you." He stepped up behind me then slipped his arms around my waist. "This changes nothing."

"If you say so," I said, crossing my arms across my breasts. I was upset and trippin' with Parker for no reason at all. It wasn't his fault Jessica was back. Plus, he had offered to give me her spot. I guess deep inside I felt he could have offered me more. I decided to let it go and let the cards fall however they chose. Turning around, I faced him and said, "It's fine, boo. Business is business."

Chapter 17

Nathaniel seemed pleasantly surprised to have me back in the training room and under his supervision. He looked like a teenage boy with a high school crush when I strolled into the training room. "Welcome back," he smiled brightly.

"Thank you. Thank you."

"Where is Jamel?" I asked, observing that Nathaniel and I were alone.

"He's in HR," he explained. "For a meeting."

My radar instinctively went up from this information. "Really?" I asked.

"I wonder what for," I said, trying to see if Nathaniel had a clue as to why Jamel needed to meet with HR.

"I'm not sure," he said, "but I'm sure it's something basic, or it could be for a job assignment. Elena has been using him in HR a lot lately."

I was pleased that Jamel had been working with Elena and thought at that moment that his frequent job assignments in her department were only going to benefit me in the long run.

"This has been the most unusual class I have ever had," Nathaniel commented.

"What do you mean?"

"My interns have spent more time outside of class than actually with me."

"Feeling jealous?" I teased. "Lonely?"

"No," he laughed. "Just stating a fact."

"That's the great thing about corporate America," I told him. "You never know what might unfold, and there is never a dull moment."

*****

According to Nathaniel, Jamel was going home for the rest of the day and would be on paid leave. I wrote his disappearance off as a virus or bug.

Working with Nathaniel, I discovered he was a Detroit native and a single parent to a two-year-old daughter named Kaitlyn, whose mother died during childbirth. He told me he and Kaitlyn's mother had been high school sweethearts, and they met their junior year. She was the straight-A honor roll student who was president of the Honor Society, and he was the school-skipping bad boy. "She turned me around," he said. "She helped me get my grades up and apply for colleges. She was my angel and my inspiration." Hearing him talk about the woman brought tears to my eyes. Nathaniel also told me he was a member of Alpha Phi Alpha fraternity and that his next move at G&L was to hopefully secure a position in the Marketing Department.

"The chair for VP is open, and I plan to make it mine," he said proudly. "I've been working on something that will prove I can handle the position."

"Your proposal?" I asked.

"Yep."

"Good luck," I told him sincerely. "I'm sure Parker is going to love it."

"I hope so."

We sat side by side on the patio of the cafeteria discussing one of my favorite sports, basketball. It felt good to laugh and kick it with a man just as friends. I was able to laugh and joke with Parker, too, but the two of us were intense. There were always hormones raging when I was in his presence. My feelings for Nathaniel were the exact opposite. I liked Nathaniel and thought he was a cutie, but I wasn't feeling him on a sexual level. Nathaniel reminded me of some of my homeboys back home that I used to hang out with whenever I went home from college for break. We would drink, smoke, and just be on plain stupid shit, back before life became so much more complicated. Thinking about those days made me homesick. I made a mental note to pay my Grams and my city a visit the next opportunity I had.

"I don't care what you say," Nathaniel laughed. "Detroit is still my team."

"They used to be mine, too," I joked, "when they were actually winning!"

"See? You one of *those* type of fans," he said, shaking his finger at me. "You're down as long as we're bringing home the rings, but then when hard times hit, you're burning a brother's jersey and jumping on team Lebron!"

We both laughed.

"Nobody likes a loser, Nate." I turned around and saw Parker standing behind us. He stood with his hands stuffed in his pants pockets, eyeing the two of us.

"This is true," Nathaniel said, wiping his hands with his napkin, "but even the best winners take a loss from time to time."

"I don't believe in taking losses." Parker laughed, staring at me. "When I make up my mind to get something, I get it. And there is nothing or no one," he said, turning his attention to Nathaniel, "that can stop me. Winning is my only option."

In that moment, I felt like a sixteen-year-old girl that had been caught by her boyfriend in the high school cafeteria with another boy. The look in Parker's eyes and in is voice was straight crazy. It occurred to me that no matter how successful and fine a man might be, he can still have his own level of insecurities and jealousy.

"Well, I'll let the two of you enjoy your lunch," Parker said. "I just wanted to let the two of you know we will have an emergency staff meeting."

"What's going on?" I asked, curious.

"Nothing to be concerned about," Parker said. "Just some staffing changes."

"A good announcement or a bad one?" I probed. In my heart, I felt the company was secure and stable, but I did

not like corporate surprises. Many large corp
soaring high one hour and bankrupt in the next.

"It depends on what side of the table you're sitting o
he said.

*****

Two hours later, the cafeteria at G&L had row after row of chairs lined up with staff members chatting, waiting to hear Parker's big announcement. I sat on the second row in between Nathaniel and Joel, one of the associates from the Ad Department. There was a large podium with microphone and audio speakers in the front of the room standing in front of a wide projection screen that had been lowered from the ceiling.

Parker sat in the front of the room to the left of the podium with a well-dressed woman sitting on his right. I asked Nathaniel who she was, and he informed me that the woman's name was Diana Smartt, and she was part of the Employee Ethics Committee.

"I don't know what's going on," he said, "but it has to be major if Diana is in the office."

"Maybe she just wanted to visit," I said.

"I doubt it."

"She is rarely ever present at staff meetings unless someone is getting promoted or—worse—someone has been booted."

"Could be your lucky day." I smiled, giving him a slight nudge in the side.

He smiled back at me. "I can only hope."

I spotted Jessica sitting in the row behind Parker and the woman. Her eyes were locked in my direction, and she had a smile plastered on her face from ear to ear. I knew being Parker's right-hand woman, she had already been informed of the big news.

I scanned the room, looking at all the warm bodies filling the seats. There was a color to represent almost every known race. G&L was truly a melting pot. Turning back toward the front of the room, I saw Parker watching me as he approached the podium. I smiled at him and then discreetly winked my eye.

"Good afternoon," he said, removing the wireless microphone from its stand.

A roar of "Hello" and "Good afternoon" came from the crowd.

"I won't keep you long," he said, speaking into the microphone. "I know we all have to get back to doing what we do best, continuing to make G&L number one."

Cheers and applause came from the crowd.

"It saddens me to inform you that after ten years with the company, Elena Toney will no longer be our director of Human Resources."

There was an uproar of moans, groans, and other reactions from the crowd. I, on the other hand, was smiling like child on Christmas morning!

"Ms. Toney is leaving to pursue other career interests," Parker continued. "We wish her the best in her endeavors. In the meantime, any and all HR-related questions should be directed to Carmella Armstrong, the HR assistant. Thank you for all your hard work," Parker said quickly, "and enjoy the rest of your day."

I knew there was so much more to Elena's departure than what was being said. My instincts told me so. Something also told me that Jamel's sudden leave had something to do with it. No matter the reason was for Elena's resignation, I was happy as a tick about the witch being out of my way. Jessica had returned, but Elena was gone. *This day is gonna turn out better than I thought,*

* * * * *

That night, Parker and I sat in my living room, cuddled up on the sofa watching movies.

"What's the real reason Elena left?" I asked.

"I really shouldn't discuss it with you," he said.

"You really shouldn't be here with me," I reminded him, "but you are."

"Point taken," he said, sighing. "Elena was given the choice to resign or be terminated."

I sat up and stared at him. "Terminated?" I asked. "For what?"

"Sexual harassment."

"What?" I asked, baffled. "For sexually harassing who?"

"Jamel Harston."

I immediately began laughing and continued to do so until I saw how serious Parker looked. "You're serious?" I asked calmly.

"Yes."

"Who made the claim?"

"He did," Parker stated. "She admitted to it and took full responsibility."

"Is that why he's out on leave?" I asked.

"Yes," Parker said, exhaling.

"Wow" was the only response I could spit out. I wanted to tell Parker that Jamel had pushed up on Elena from day one, but I kept this information to myself. In my mind, I wondered why Jamel had thrown Elena under the bus. That was supposed to be my responsibility. I had a nagging sensation there was more to the story.

Chapter 18

The day had finally arrived for Jamel or myself to be awarded a full-time position with G&L. I was ready and felt like the only thing standing between me and the $40,000 a year promotion was the time that Nathaniel was taking to make the announcement. Jamel and I had barely spoken since his return, and that was fine by me. I still had evidence of his dirty-ass secret, but Elena was gone, and I was content with that.

To commemorate what I knew was going to be a joyous occasion, I had chosen to wear my red Dolce & Gabbana pantsuit that Parker had purchased for me.

"The two of you are going to excel no matter what you choose to do," Nathaniel said, standing in the front of the room. "I wish I could hire you both, but there is only one position open. We considered many factors when making this decision," he said, "and both of you came with high recommendations—so high that I consulted Mr. Bryant and asked him to make the final selection."

I knew the job was mine after hearing Parker's name. When it came to me and Jamel, I was Parker's favorite.

"Now, without wasting any more time," Nathaniel said, "I'd like to welcome Jamel on board as G&L's newest ad sales associate."

I felt like I had been punched in the stomach and then stomped on after hitting the ground. I was shocked and pissed.

"Congratulations, Jamel," Nathaniel said, shaking his hand.

"Excuse me?" I said, marching toward the door. "Congrats, Jamel," I said before stomping out of the room.

* * * * *

"May I help you, Asia?" Jessica asked as I pushed through the office doors.

"Is he in?"

"Yes, but he's busy," she stated, jumping up out of her chair.

If there was ever a time for her not to get in my way, this was it. "This won't take long," I said, angry.

"You can't come barging in here," Jessica stated, standing in between me and Parker's door.

"I just did!" I snapped. "Now move!"

The two of us went back and forth for a few seconds until I came to the conclusion that I was going to have to beat her ass.

Fortunately for her, Parker opened his door before I made my move. "Let her in," he said to Jessica.

"What?" she asked, turning to look at him.

"You heard him," I said, pushing by her.

"Parker…"Jessica started.

"Hold my calls," he said, cutting her off.

Jessica's mouth was still open as Parker closed the door in her face.

"You want to tell me why Jamel is still on the payroll and I'm officially unemployed?" I asked, getting right to the point. My heart was beating a mile a minute, pounding in my ears.

"If you are referring to my decision to select him for the ad sales position," he began, "you need to know that several factors went into that decision."

I said nothing and arched an eyebrow at him, prodding him to explain further.

"Work history, for one," he said. "Then there was a high recommendation from Adam Wales, and—"

"I bet! Adam Wales gave him that recommendation 'cause Jamel's fucking him!" I blurted.

Parker looked stunned from the knowledge I had just dropped.

I was pissed to the fullest, and there was no one protected from my wrath. "You know, maybe if *I* was fucking Adam, I'd have the damn job, but I am not into strap-ons."

"Watch your mouth!" he ordered.

"You are a liar," I snapped. "Anything I asked for? Whatever I like?" I said, repeating his words. "You are such a liar!" I said shaking my head.

"You never asked for that position," he said bluntly.

When I thought about it, I realized he was right. I had never come out and asked him for that particular position. Still, the fact that he was right only further infuriated me.

"So I'm a liar?" he asked. "I never lied to you about anything. You, on the other hand, have been lying since day one," he continued, walking toward me. "Elise has never even heard of you, and I'm willing to bet your letters of recommendation were fabricated."

I was busted and had no response to his accusations, which were all true of course.

"So again, I ask, how am I the liar?"

"Whatever," I said, turning on my heels. I opened his office door and found Jessica eavesdropping, which I half-expected. "Move," I said through clenched teeth.

Giving me a small smirk, she stepped out of my path.

I pushed the doors open so hard they rattled and stepped into the hall. I could hear someone calling my name. Ignoring the voice, I continued to the elevator and then, as soon as the doors opened, I walked on.

* * * * *

Staring at my packed luggage sitting on the floor in front of me, I tried to come up with a plan. I knew that the few grand I had in my account would be gone within months if I stayed in Atlanta. There was only one logical solution. I needed to go home.

"Hello?" My grandmother's voice sounded like it radiated over the phone.

"Hi, Grams," I said, trying hard to disguise my anger and frustration.

"Asia, baby!" she said. "How you doing?"

"I'm fine, Grams. How are you?" I asked.

"Not bad, baby," she said, coughing lightly. "Livin'."

"I miss you."

"I miss you too."

"And I wanted to let you know I'll probably be there to visit soon." I started to tell her why, but I didn't want her to worry.

"Take your time, baby," she said gently. "I know you gotta work."

I wish, I thought to myself.

There was a loud knock at my front door.

"Parker," I whispered aloud.

"Say what, baby?" Grams asked.

"Nothing, Grams," I said tenderly. "I have to go now, but I love you."

"Love you, too, Asia."

"See you soon," I said, blowing her a kiss over the phone.

"Bye, baby."

* * * * *

There was another knock on the door, followed by the doorbell ringing.

"Why don't you just use the key?!" I asked, swinging the door open.

"I didn't know I was supposed to have one," Nathaniel

said lightly.

"What are you doing here?" I asked. "And how did you get this address?"

"I'm here to make sure you're alright," he said. "Jessica gave it to me. I tried to stop you at the office, but you kept going," he said.

"Come in," I invited. exhaling deeply.

"This is a really nice place," he said, looking around the room. "How much they paying ya'll now to be an intern?"

"Thanks. It belongs to a friend," I said, plopping back down on the sofa. "Have a seat."

Easing down on the sofa next to me he nodded toward my luggage. "Are you leaving?" he asked, staring at my bags.

"Yeah. I'm going back home."

"So, one turn-down, and you're just giving up?" he asked.

"I'm not giving up. I'm just—"

"Giving up," he said. "G&L is not the only marketing firm in this city."

"I know," I said, "but it is the best."

"So find another one," he suggested, "and help make them better."

"You have an answer for everything," I said, sighing.

"But you're reconsidering," he said. "Aren't you?"

"Maybe," I said, sucking my teeth.

He elbowed me lightly in the side, causing me to giggle.

"Ticklish?" he asked, digging his fingers into my sides lightly.

"Stooop!" I laughed lightly. "Nate!" I continued to giggle until he finally let me go. Collapsing on the sofa, I inhaled deeply, attempting to catch my breath.

"You alright?" he asked, leaning over me.

"Yes, "I said, exhaling loudly. I closed my eyes and then threw my hand against my head. "I'm fine." Although I had a million thoughts and then some running through my mind, it felt good to laugh. "I'll be even better once I figure out what I'm going to do."

"Asia..." Nathaniel said seriously.

"Yes?"

"Stay," he said. "You really never know what's in God's plan for you here."

"I wish He would just tell me," I said, "or give me a hint or something. No, scratch that," I said. "I need direct instructions. I've never been good with hints, and—"

Nate silenced my words with his lips. I jumped at first, but then I felt that little burning in the pit of my stomach that told me my body was getting turned on. Nathaniel's lips were soft and full and felt so damn good against mine. Slipping my hands up around his neck, I pulled him closer. Sucking my bottom lip slowly, Nathaniel slipped his hand underneath me, pulling me down further on the sofa. Positioning his body in between my legs, he moved his lips from mine, to my forehead, to my chin, and then to my neck. My pussy jumped every time he kissed a different area, and my heart fluttered.

"Wait," I said softly.

Nathaniel instantly sat back on the sofa away from me.

Sitting up, I looked at him. He was really a beautiful man. Standing to my feet, I extended my hand to him.

Lying on my back, I shook slightly from Nathaniel's touch. His hand massaged my ankle gently as he licked and then sucked each of my toes. Making a slow trail from my ankle up my calf to my thigh, he blew softly. The warmth of his breath against my skin sent chills scrambling over my body. Grabbing the back of my thighs, Nathaniel held my legs open as his mouth met my lower lips and his tongue explored my hottest pressure point. Shaking uncontrollably, I bit my bottom lip to keep from screaming as my cream trickled from in between my legs. Moving up slowly, he pushed my breasts together with his hands and then sucked my protruding nipples at the same time. After exploring every inch of my body with his hands and mouth, Nathaniel finally entered me. I squeezed the muscles of my pussy tightly, latching onto his thick dick like I had the jaws of life in between my thighs. He massaged my pussy with his dick as our lips and tongues explored each other until we each reached the joyous point of climax.

Kissing him slowly on the lips, I smiled. Stepping back, he looked at me for what had to be the one-hundredth time in the last hour. He smiled and grabbed the belt of the robe I was wearing and then pulled me back into his arms. Squeezing me tightly, he ran his fingers through my hair. After the two of us connected sexually, we showered and then lay in bed, nose to nose, staring into each other's eyes in silence. It was one of the most intimate moments I had ever experienced—one I instantly looked forward to sharing with Nathaniel again.

"I'll call you," he said, finally pulling away.

"You better," I said, kissing him again.

The two of us had changed things between us, and I liked the place I felt I was in with him at that moment.

"Bye, beautiful," he said before walking away.

I waited for him to climb into his Escalade and drive off before I began to shut the door. The loud roar of an engine, followed by screeching and screaming of brakes made me stop. I cracked the door open and saw the taillights of a Ferrari California as the car sped around the corner.

Chapter 19

Running my hands down the front of my skirt, I casually checked my reflection in the office window. I looked like the baddest bitch that ever rocked a suit and heels. My short black jacket contoured to my upper body, while my straight skirt accentuated my legs. I wore open-toe stilettos with the ensemble, which was conservative but still sexy. I was taking Nathaniel's advice; I was not giving up. I was going to land my position at G&L or ruin Parker's career trying. I knew exposing my affair with Parker would put me on blast as well, but it was something I was willing to risk.

I took a deep breath then pushed and then pushed the doors to the executive conference room open. "Good morning," I said with a smile, looking around the room.

Parker sat at the head of the table. He looked calm and not at all surprised by my arrival. Around the table sat an unfamiliar face, along with Nathaniel and Bill the marketing supervisor and Jonah, the ad sales vice president.

"Sorry I'm late," I said, easing down in the chair next to Parker. Flashing my eyes down the table at Nathaniel,

I smiled slightly. I could see the question *"What are you doing here?"* in his eyes. I hated that Nathaniel was present, but it was too late to turn back.

"It's not a problem, Asia," Parker said smoothly. "We're just getting started."

I looked at him, and he looked completely unshaken by my presence, as if he had predicted I'd be there.

"Armando, this is Asia Turner," Parker said. He was looking over at the stranger sitting to the left of him.

"It's nice to meet you, Asia," Armando said in a deep baritone voice. The man was an older brother with dark skin and gray cat-like eyes. Much like Parker, he wore a dark tailored suit that I recognized as Armani.

"You as well," I said cordially.

"Asia, it's really a good thing you're here," Parker said, cuffing his fingers together.

"Oh really?"

"Yes," Parker said. "I know you wanted to wait until later to present your proposal, but I think now is as good a time as any."

I was confused as to what proposal he was referring to, but I smiled anyway. "My proposal?" I said, trying to remain calm. "Well, Parker, I didn't come prepared. I apologize," I said. "Had I known, I would have gotten things together."

"It's okay, Asia," Parker said, looking over at me. "I came prepared for the both of us." Sliding a small folder across the table to me, Parker asked, "Would you like me to begin?"

I nodded my head. Opening the folder, I scanned over the information: a four-million-dollar contract. The layout and info had my name at the top, but I had never seen the information in my life.

"Take one and pass them around," Parker advised the other men as he handed out presentation folders. "Armando, when Asia came to me with her plan on how G&L could double your clientele and help increase your profits 85 percent, I was somewhat skeptical."

I continued to read over the information as Parker gave the man background on how I allegedly came up with an innovative campaign for his company. I smiled and agreed with Parker, occasionally throwing out a fact from time to time from the paper in front of me. I have a personal motto: "Fake it till you make it." That's exactly what my ass was doing.

"I like what I've heard here today," Armando said. "Asia, you did a great job with this proposal."

"Thank you, Armando," I smiled. The proposal was banging, and Parker had outdone himself with it. I couldn't believe he was letting me take the credit for his work. Then I remembered I was living in his residence and had enough information and evidence to have his ass fired for fraternizing with an employee. Looking up, my eyes locked with Nathaniel's. We stared at each other until he finally turned his head. I wondered if now that the two of us had slept together things might become awkward.

"Gentlemen, I'll see you in the cafeteria in twenty

minutes," Parker said, looking around the table. "Asia, I'd like to see you in my office. Now," he ordered.

* * * * *

"What is she doing here?" Jessica asked as she watched me following Parker through the office doors.

"Go downstairs and wait for me," he told her.

"Parker, I—"

"This is not up for discussion," he barked. "I'll see you downstairs."

Jessica's face turned slightly red as she instantly closed her mouth. Snatching her purse off the desk, she frowned at me before stomping out of the office. There was a part of me that wanted her to stay simply because I had never seen this side of Parker, and I have to admit it had me a little scared.

As soon as the two of us stepped behind closed doors, he grabbed me by my neck and pushed me against the wall. "Don't you ever talk to me in front of another employee like you did yesterday," he said. His voice was calm but commanding. "Do you understand?" he asked.

"Yes."

"Do you love him?"

I knew he was referring to Nathaniel, but considering the circumstances and the fact that with one wrong move Parker could permanently cut off my air supply, I decided to play dumb. "Love who?" I asked.

"Don't play with me, Asia," he said through clenched

teeth. He applied slight pressure to my neck, enough to encourage me to lie.

"No," I said softly. The truth was I felt something for Nathaniel that I had never felt before, and yes I did think I was falling for the man, but there was no way I was gonna admit that.

"Good," he said, "because I refuse to share your heart."

Easing his grip on my neck, Parker kissed me hard on the mouth before pushing me face down on the desk. I flinched slightly as he ran his hand up my skirt and pulled my panties to the side. I wasn't ready when he slammed his dick in me from the back, and I didn't want it. However, I bit my lip and allowed him to have his way. In that moment, I knew that I had started a vicious game with Parker, and I had to be the one to end it if I planned on winning and surviving.

*****

Thirty minutes later, Parker stood at the podium again in front of a cafeteria full of associates. I stood against the wall close to the podium, looking over the crowd. Nathaniel sat in the first row with his hands clasped together. He looked up at me with a blank stare.

I smiled affectionately and then frowned when he looked away without returning my smile. *What is his problem?* I thought to myself.

"As you all know, here at G&L, we believe in going against the traditional grain," Parker spoke into the microphone.

"We take chances and intelligent risks. We believe that greatness is acquired through diligence and dedication. We take the ordinary and weave it and mold it into something extraordinary."

While he paused briefly, everyone in the room clapped, including me.

"As you all know, our marketing team is one of the most aggressive in the industry," he stated. "They have a history of taking what is considered small fish and turning it into big bass."

There was laughter throughout the room.

"However, lately our fishermen and fisherwomen," he said, encouraged by laughter once again, "have been without a captain. In looking for the right person to fill the position, I decided we needed someone bold and full of zest."

I looked at Jessica. She was practically bouncing out of her chair with excitement. I looked at Nathaniel, and his demeanor had changed slightly. I could tell he was anxious to see if he had gotten the position. I wondered how many other people in the room were wishing and praying for the same thing.

"A go-getter with a proven track record of getting the job done," Parker continued, "by any means necessary. So, without further adieu, ladies and gentleman, I proudly present to you, G&L's new VP of marketing," he said, loudly.

I watched as Jessica sat up with her feet planted firmly.

I felt bad for Nathaniel; it was obvious to me just looking at the woman that she had been promoted to the position.

"Asia Turner," Parker called out.

What? I asked myself. I thought my ears were playing tricks on me until I looked over and saw that the blank stare had returned to Nathaniel's face.

"Asia," Parker said, looking over at the wall where I was standing, "come on up."

I eased out of my chair and slowly began walking up to the podium. The crowd stood up and began clapping loudly. I even heard a few whistles from the back of the room. I was dazed and damn confused as Parker handed me an envelope that had been lying on the podium.

"You'll have to excuse Asia," he said, laughing lightly. "She's a little shy."

He and I both knew I'm by no means shy. Hell, I was shocked! There is a very big difference.

"Would you like to say a few words?" he asked, staring at me.

Hell, I'd like to say a lot of them, I thought to myself.

"I'd just like to say I am honored to be part of this illustrious firm," I said slowly, enunciating every word like I was reading a queue card. I know I probably sounded like an idiot. I wanted to take that microphone and go across Parker's head with it. He had put me on the spot for the second time that morning. "I can't wait to get to know all of you," I said humbly. "Um, thank you." I smiled and then nodded my head. I looked at Parker with raised eyebrows as I handed him the microphone.

"Well, folks," Parker said, "let's get back to work. Thanks, team." Then he turned to me and whispered, "Congratulations, superstar."

I was bum-rushed by associates and members of management shaking my hand and congratulating me. Everything felt like it was moving in a blur. I snapped out of my mental state of shock and managed to speak coherently when Parker introduced me to the three members of the board of directors.

"Congrats, baby girl, "Oscar said, pushing his way through the crowd. "I told you good thangs come out of the mailroom."

"Thank you, Oscar," I said sweetly. I saw Nathaniel standing in the distance looking like he had lost his best friend. I smiled and excused my way to the place where he was standing. "Nate, I—"

"Congratulations, Asia." He smiled faintly and then shook my hand. "I'm sure you'll do a great job." He turned and walked away before I could explain that I knew nothing about Parker appointing me to the position.

I could feel someone watching me. Looking to my left, I saw Jessica standing in the corner. Her blues eyes were zoomed in on me like a radar gun on a traffic speeder. I wondered if Parker had her spying on Nathaniel and me. I was so confused, and I didn't know what to think. I opened the envelope that Parker had given me and found a congratulations card with a hundred-dollar gift card and a set of keys.

"The keys are to your office," Parker said, coming up from behind me. "Meet me there in fifteen minutes."

*****

My office was located on the fourth floor, secluded from the other associates. It wasn't as big as Parker's, and I didn't have my own private bathroom, but it was nice, and it was mine! Leaning back in the big leather desk chair, I exhaled. There was a huge bouquet of red roses sitting on the corner of the mahogany desk. There was no card, but I already knew who sent them.

When a knock came on the door, I said loudly, "Enter!" I smiled faintly when I saw Parker coming through the door.

"How does it feel?" he asked, sitting on the edge of the desk.

"I'm still in total disbelief," I admitted.

"This is what you wanted," he said, "and you got it."

"How did you manage to pull this off?"

"Let me worry about that," he said. "You just focus on doing a good job."

"I will."

"I'll get you information on what contracts we are currently trying to secure. I'll also get you a list of important contacts you'll need to know," he said. "HR will get you updated and changed over in the system. You and I will go over the financial details later."

The mere mention of money grabbed my attention.

"Later when?" I asked.

"Tonight over dinner," he said. "That is, if you don't already have plans."

I wanted to see Nathaniel again, but our celebration would have to wait. I felt a certain obligation to entertain Parker, at least for the night. "No plans," I said, smiling sweetly.

"I'll pick you up at nine tonight," he said, extending his open arms to me.

I did not want to get out of my chair. There was a small part of me that felt like it was all a dream I would wake up from at any moment. However, I stood and allowed him to hold me in his arms.

"Your name will be on the door by morning," he whispered as he pressed his face against my neck. "Things are about to take a dramatic turn for you, Asia. I hope you do not make me regret the decisions I have made thus far concerning us."

Pulling back, I looked in his eyes. I saw passion and lust and something else I couldn't put my finger on—something that inflicted fear in me and shook me to my inner core. "I promise you that you won't regret it," I said soothingly.

Cupping my face with his hands, Parker leaned in and kissed me hard on the mouth. I returned his kiss with joy and excitement. My feelings of pleasure at that moment were not from physical satisfaction, but rather because I knew my time had finally come and I was on my way to the top.

*****

I was sitting behind my new desk going over the contracts Parker had given me when Nathaniel knocked on my door. "Hey you," I said gently. "Come in."

He stepped through the door and then stopped.

"Are you okay?" I asked, genuinely concerned about his feelings.

"I'm just…well, just confused," he said, stuffing his hands down in his pockets.

"About?"

"Last night, I thought we shared something," he said, looking at me. "I thought the two of us had a real connection."

"Me too," I said happily.

"Don't patronize me, Asia," he snapped. "I understand how the game goes. I just expected more from you, that's all."

"What do you mean, the game?"

"I thought you were so much better than that."

"What are you talking about?"

"Don't play dumb, Asia. You knew that proposal you presented to Armando was mine,"

"Nate, I didn't—"

"Save it, Asia," he said. "You sat right there and took credit for something that wasn't yours. You took credit for what was mine. Hell, I woulda respected you more if you had told me what you were about," he said. "You'd still be triflin' as hell, but at least I would have respected you for bein' honest."

On any normal day I would have retaliated, even if I did appear to be in the wrong, but this was no normal day. I sat speechless, trying hard to swallow the lump that had developed in my throat.

"You can give this to Parker from me," Nathaniel said, removing an envelope from his jacket pocket. He dropped it on my desk and said, "It's my letter of resignation."

"Nate, you can't quit!" I said standing and walking around the desk.

"I just did," he said. He walked out my office with me directly on his heels.

"Nate, talk to me," I said desperately. "Please."

"Good luck, Asia," he said, staring at the floor. "I wish you the best."

The urge to throw my arms around him and beg him to stay was there, but my pride was stronger. I stepped back and turned, walking in the opposite direction. With each step, it felt like my heart was breaking.

I looked up and saw Parker at the other end of the hall. He looked pleased from what he obviously had seen take place between Nathaniel and myself. Shaking my head, I reentered my office and slammed the door.

Chapter 20

One month later

They say "to whom much is given, much is required." That's the damn truth. Since being appointed as VP of marketing, I was constantly on the move. G&L had a wide array of clients from all walks of life—from athletes, to actresses, to authors, to large retail outlets, to big-name corporations, to small business owners. My marketing team worked hard to get them and even harder to keep them. Parker explained that G&L had no international clients, and I advised him that would change now that I was onboard. He loved my ambition, but I knew what he loved even more was the way I sexed him up. For my part, our love affair had become old and was tainted with so much deception that I could no longer enjoy it. Part of me wanted—no, *needed*—it to be over, but Parker refused to let go, and I didn't push him to. There were times when I felt like I was dangling on strings and Parker was the puppet master. If I didn't play my role just right, he would cut the strings and let me crumble to the ground while he snatched everything from beneath me that was holding me up.

As for the position I was appointed to, I was welcomed with open arms by those under my immediate guidance and received few to no questions about my work history or qualifications. The associates at G&L had been trained to not question Parker's decisions, and they practiced what they were taught well. The board of directors trusted Parker to no avail and stood by him. They were by his side in war and in victory.

I had officially made history with the company. At twenty-four, I was the youngest VP in G&L history, not to mention the first woman. My new position came with a $6,000 signing bonus, a yearly bonus of 10 percent of the company's annual earnings (contingent upon the company doing well as a whole, as well as meeting a list of criteria set by the owners), and an annual starting salary of $85,000. When Parker went over the numbers and figures with me, I cried sincere tears.

I finally purchased my own car, a 2011 red Mercedes Benz. I also started paying Grams back for all my years of free loading. Tracey and I were still not on speaking terms. I missed her like crazy, and my life and money were finally all good. I wanted to share all those exciting life changes with my bestie, but pride would not allow me to make the first move.

Parker assisted me with finding a mortgage company that would approve and finance me (a slightly difficult thing to do because I didn't have the mandatory work history). I moved out of his brownstone and purchased my first home in a beautiful community called Carriage Park. I had four bedrooms and three and a half baths all to myself, and I loved it! Dana, the realtor that assisted me, loved working with me and said I was the easiest client she'd ever dealt with; I knew what I wanted, and I did the math on what I could afford. I was finally living the life that others only dreamt or read about. Life was good, but I always found some area where it could be improved even more.

*****

I had been researching a company called Ojima Motors. It had started in Tokyo but had opened four plants across the U.S. within the last three years. Originally, all of their marketing and advertising was handled in-house, but I wanted them on G&L's client list and was determined that I would make them one of our next major contracts.

"Asia, Michio Ojima has turned down every firm that has ever approached him for his business," Parker explained.

The two of us sat in his office, along with Jonah and Jessica, as I presented my idea to approach Mr. Ojima for business. Jessica sat in the corner quietly taking notes as Parker, Jonah, and I went back and forth.

"So you're saying it can't be done?" I asked, crossing my legs.

"I'm not saying it can't," he said. "I would never tell you that." His eyes traveled from mine down to my legs then slowly back up. "I'm saying it has not been done thus far," He continued.

I frowned, giving him a cut-it-out look.

"We've approached him before, and each time the answer has been 'no'. He won't even agree to meet with us," Jonah added.

"Each of those times has been before me," I said confidently. "If you don't mind me saying so, I think I bring something new and fresh to the table."

Jessica cleared her throat, then laughed lightly. Her attitude had been a little stank since Parker had appointed me as VP. *It's been four damn weeks,* I thought. *It's time for that jealous bitch to build a bridge and move on or get knocked off into the damn river.* The decision was hers either way, but if she continued to try my patience, I was going to make it very hard for her, and I could have guaranteed she wouldn't like the end result. At first I thought it was Parker who was co-dependent upon her, but the more I got to know her, the more I saw that their dependency went both ways. He needed someone to organize his work life and time, and she needed to be needed. She appeared to be the perfect candidate for his assistant, and she did her job well.

"Jessica, would you like to add something to the conversation?" I asked, staring at her. Her blue eyes grew wide.

Damn straight I'm calling you out, I thought.

"Why would you waste your time on a fish that won't bite?" she asked, looking at me. "It's a waste of time and money."

I respected her for speaking up, but I wasn't about to back down. "Because it's a damn big fish," I said, "and it's not a waste of time or money if you use the right bait the first time."

"You heard what Jonah said," she said. "They've never even agreed to a meeting. You're trying to beat a dead horse, and it's not going to happen," she said, exhaling.

"What if I told you I already have a meeting in line?" I asked, looking at Parker.

He studied my facial expression and then leaned forward in his chair. "I would ask you when you were going to tell me," he said, giving me a stern look.

"I have a meeting scheduled with Ojima," I said, smiling.

"Are you serious?" Jonah asked, looking from me to Parker then back at me.

"I don't play when it comes to money," I told him, and I was dead serious.

"When are they coming?" Parker asked, shaking his head.

"In two weeks," I said proudly, "but they're not coming here. We're going to Japan."

"Excellent," Jonah said, standing. "Parker, I have another meeting to attend, but let me know when and the details. Good job, Asia." He smiled before walking out.

"So the company is dishing out a free trip for you to get a no?" Jessica blurted out. "No way."

What she didn't realize was that she was about to dive

in that river head first without warning.

"The company is providing transportation for Jonah and myself to secure our biggest contract all year," I said, cutting my eyes at her. "We will let you know when we need a memo to be sent. Until then, leave securing deals and decision-making to those who hold the titles to do so."

Her face turned a pale shade of red. I was ready and waiting for her to respond, but she didn't get the chance.

"Jessica, give Asia and myself a moment alone," Parker instructed her.

"Certainly," she said sweetly. She flashed me a cunning smile, an indication that she thought she had won.

I watched as she switched out the office, shutting the door behind her. "What is her problem?" I asked.

"She's been my assistant for six years," he said. "She knows what I've been through to build G&L to what it is right now. She doesn't want to see me make unnecessary mistakes. She's just cautious."

"She's a bitch, and you need to check her," I snapped.

"Asia, you're taking things too personally," he said calmly.

"Oh? Am I?" I asked, standing.

"Yes."

"Well, let me get back to business," I said with attitude, "and strictly business is where it will stay from here on out." I was having a temper tantrum, and yes there was a hidden message in my words that went something like this: *"From here on out, all this ass is off limits! How's that for not taking shit personal?"*

"Asia," Parker said softly, "don't act like that. I didn't mean—"

"Oh, don't worry about it," I said, waving my hand in the air. "I'm over here trying to prove that I deserve this position, trying to make you proud, while you let Girl Friday out there get out of place and disrespect me."

"Asia, you're blowing this whole thing out of proportion," he said, attempting to reason with me.

He was right. I was blowing it out of proportion, but I knew if I did, he would eventually give in and see things my way. It didn't matter how long Parker had been dealing with me, I could still use tears and frustration to get my way.

"Well, that will be the only thing I'm blowing," I whispered. "I'll call Mr. Ojima and let him know we no longer need to meet because my CEO's personal assistant, in all her infinite wisdom, said it would be a waste of money."

"Asia, you're being childish," he said. "Sit down and talk to me."

"I have work to do," I said, opening the door. "Thanks for listening."

The triumphant smile on Jessica's face was the first thing I saw as I exited Parker's office. I gave her a look that dared her to say something to me.

"Asia and Jessica, can I speak to you for a moment?" Parker said loudly.

I stopped my stride and then turned to see him standing in his office doorway.

"Sure," Jessica said happily, stepping by me.

I was surprised she didn't break out in a skip on her way to Parker's office. I sighed loudly and followed behind her.

"Both of you sit down," Parker ordered. Once we were both seated Parker came and stood in front of the desk. "I think we should establish some ground rules," he said. "Actually, there's just one. Jessica, I expect you to show Asia the same respect you show the other officers and associates."

The stunned expression on her face was priceless.

"When we are in a meeting, I expect you to refrain from any outbursts or any form of expression exhibiting your disapproval."

Jessica couldn't say a word.

"Do we have an understanding?" he asked.

She remained silent but nodded her head.

"Great." Parker looked at me, and I nodded my head as well. "Jessica, please make hotel and flight accommodations for three departing on—"

"The twenty-fifth," I answered, completing his sentence.

"The twenty-fifth," Parker repeated. "Remember to get reservations for three."

"Okay," she said, standing. "But for three? Who else is going?" she asked.

"Asia, Jonah, and myself," Parker informed her.

I suppressed my smile, but I was happy I was not going in to meet Mr. Ojima alone. I had scheduled the meeting, but despite my display of confidence, deep down inside I was nervous as hell about securing the contract.

"Would you like me to accompany the three of you?" she asked slowly.

"That won't be necessary," Parker informed her. "Just work out all the details before we leave."

"I'll make accommodations," she said before leaving.

I waited until Parker had the door closed and then turned to him. "Thank you," I said sweetly.

"The attitude is gone just like that?" he said, rubbing my back.

"Just like that," I whispered.

"You're easy to please," he whispered, trailing kisses down my neck. "I told you, whatever you need, just ask and it shall be granted."

I didn't need or want Parker to give me anything. I planned to get and fund everything I wanted on my own, and the Ojimi contract was going to give me the security I needed.

* * * * *

I decided to finally break down and call Tracey. She answered on the first ring and sounded genuinely happy to hear from me. I asked if she wanted to hang out, and she agreed. I decided to treat her to dinner and martinis at Ruth's Chris. I sat finishing off my first black cherry-tinis while Tracey nursed her fourth. The two of us had just finished eating a dinner of steak and lobster and were discussing my upcoming trip.

"I'm so jealous," she said, rolling her eyes. "Harold has got to step his game up."

"How are you two doing?" I asked. It was the first time the entire night that we had discussed their marriage and the incident that led to us not speaking for over a month.

"We're okay," she said. "I'm insecure as hell at times about what he's doing, but I love my husband and I'm never letting go."

"Counseling?"

"Girl, I don't need a shrink to tell me my husband fucked up and cheated," she said, smacking her lips.

"Tracey, I'm not talking about for *him*," I said. "I mean for *you*."

"What you mean for me?" she asked, pouting.

"Since ya'll started going through your rough patch, you've started drinking more," I advised her. "Then the pill-popping."

"I got this," she said. "Seriously, A."

I didn't want to push the subject or drive her away, so I let it go. I would rather have my bestie in my life with all her suppressed issues than not in my life at all.

"So, Tokyo, here you come," she said, snapping her fingers. "I'm so jealous!"

"Trace, it's a business trip." I laughed. "It is not like I'm going on vacation."

"I don't care what the reason is," she pouted. "You're still going!" she said, shaking her head.

"I'll bring you back a souvenir," I told her.

"Okay. Bring me back Mr. Ojojo's—"

"Mr. Ojima's," I corrected, shaking my head.

"Mr. O ever," she slurred. "Bring me back one of his sons. I guarantee with what they banking, a bitch ain't got to work."

"Trace, you crazy."

"I know, I know," she said, standing up from the table. "I'll be right back."

As I'd motioned for our waiter to bring me the check. I saw a familiar face standing toward the door waiting to be seated: Nathaniel. He was with an exotic-looking woman with short tapered hair. She was extremely tall, with a curvaceous figure. The two of them looked extremely happy as they laughed and talked. By the time Tracey returned to the table, I had paid the bill and dropped the waiter a tip. As the two of us were headed toward the door, Nathaniel spotted me. I smiled at him and waved. I was expecting him to throw up his middle finger, but instead he smiled back. The two of us hadn't seen each other since his resignation, but Oscar had informed me that Nathaniel had taken a VP position with Elise. I was happy for him. I missed talking to him and still replayed the one night we had shared back in my mind from time to time, but at the same time I felt he still held some ill feelings toward me and that he wanted nothing to do with me.

"Who is that? " Tracey asked, looking back at his table.

"He used to work with me," I simply said.

The two of us were out the door and halfway to my car when Nathaniel came running out. "Asia!" he called.

"Hey, Nate," I smiled. "How are you?"

"I'm good," he said. "How are you?" he asked.

"I'm doing good."

"You look great."

"Thank you," I smiled.

"Hello," Tracey said, looking from me to Nate.

"Oh, Tracey, this is Nathaniel," I said. "Nate, this Tracey."

"It's nice to meet you," he said, and the two of them shook hands.

"You too," Tracey purred. "And who is your glamorous friend you left sitting inside?" she asked.

"Tracey!" I said, elbowing her slightly.

"I'm just asking because that's a big girl," she continued. It was obvious the martinis had kicked into overdrive. "I don't mean big as in big, but she's like a beautiful Amazon queen."

I pressed unlock on my key and then gently pulled her by her arm, escorting her around to the passenger side of the car.

"Seriously, she is gorgeous," she said as I helped her get in. "But we will fight her big ass if—"

I quickly shut and locked the door. "Too many tinis," I said, shaking my head. "Sorry about that."

Nathaniel laughed. "It's cool," he said. "My sister is the same way."

"Oh, she's not my sister," I said. "Well, she's not my blood sister, but she is like a sister." I rambled.

"Well, that is my sister," he said, pointing back at the restaurant. "My blood sister."

We both laughed.

"She's beautiful," I said, smiling.

"So is yours," he said, stuffing his hands in his pockets.

I hadn't noticed before, but it was the first time I had seen him without a suit. He looked good in his baby blue Ralph Lauren polo shirt and khakis. He looked real good.

"Thank you!!" Tracey yelled, from behind the car window.

Shaking my head, I laughed. "She has really got to learn how to hold her liquor," I said.

"You are too," he said lowly.

"What?" I asked, confused. "I'm not buzzed or drunk."

"Not that," he stated. "You're beautiful."

We stared at each other for a moment until I was the first to look away. I didn't know what was going on with the flutters in my stomach or why I was feeling like a little pigtail-wearing schoolgirl, but I was in that moment.

"Aww!" Tracey yelled. "That is so effin' sweet!!"

Shaking my head, I exhaled. "Well, I better go," I said.

"Let me get your door."

I waited as he opened the door and held it open for me. "Thank you," I smiled

"I'm sorry," he whispered.

"For what?"

"About the things I said that day," he said. "I shouldn't have."

"I'm sorry, too, Nate," I said honestly. "I didn't know that proposal was yours, but I did know it wasn't mine,, and I shouldn't have taken credit. But I went to that meeting with one thing on my mind, and the whole thing got out of control, and—"

Pressing his finger to my lips, he silenced me. "Can we start over?" he asked.

"Yes!" I said eagerly.

"Call me," he said. "I miss you, Asia."

"I miss you too."

Cupping my face with his hand, Nathaniel gave me a short, sweet kiss on the lips. The kiss was innocent but enough to tell me I was still very much attracted to him.

"Talk to you later," he said. "Goodnight."

"Goodnight." I waited for him to reenter the restaurant before pulling out of the parking lot.

"He loves you, Asia," Tracey mumbled, "and I think you love him." Those were the last words she spoke before she began to snore loudly.

"I think you're right, sis," I whispered, merging onto the interstate.

Chapter 21

The trip to Tokyo took just over fourteen hours, but it was worth every second. I successfully secured my first major contract. At first, Mr. Ojima was dead set against using G&L to market his brand. In fact, it was his son Akio who had agreed to meet with me, pretending to be his father. I could see the frustration on Parker's face the moment he heard the news. "I got this," I told him.

To get Mr. Ojima to sit down and talk with me, I decided to use two of the three things I knew were a universal language: money and my feminine charm. The third would have been pussy, but I didn't want the contracts that damn bad. I used my feminine charm to stroke Mr. Ojima's ego to the point that the man actually blushed. I told him how brilliant he was and how he had created an empire that weak, easily persuaded men could never obtain. Granted, he was a family man, but he was still a man, and all men like to hear about how great and talented they are from time to time. Next, I showed him the numbers and the facts. I showed him where he stood with marketing and advertising without G&L, and then I painted a vivid picture of where he could and would be with us on his side. I brought my A game, and the end result was a multi-million-dollar contract.

* * * * *

I was going over the details of a new project I was working on when there was a knock on my door. Ten seconds later, Colleen Chambers came strolling into my office. I had met Colleen when I was first appointed to the position of VP. Colleen was the chief financial officer, the CFO, at G&L and rarely made any appearances. I liked Colleen from the moment I met her. She was a short, dark-skinned woman that looked like she was in her mid to late forties. She had a loud, contagious laugh that made everyone want to laugh just from hearing it. However, on that day she came knocking, she wasn't laughing.

"Good afternoon, Asia."

"Good afternoon, Colleen."

"How is everything going?" she asked.

"Great, thank you."

The two of us exchanged pleasantries, but I could tell from the look in Colleen's eyes that she was there to conduct official and unpleasant business.

"Please sit down," I instructed her.

"Thank you."

"Asia, I wish I was visiting under different circumstances," she said, "however, I'm here because the board has received some shocking allegations."

I tried not to show any emotion whatsoever as Colleen went into detail about the allegations and explained that there had been an ongoing investigation. There were questions about the spending and allocation of corporate funds. She knew about hotel rooms, jewelry, cash advances on the corporate credit card, and everything Parker had done for me. I listened in silence as Colleen politely explained to me that things at G&L were about to take a dramatic turn. In other words, the proverbial shit was about to hit the proverbial fan, and I was right in the middle of it.

* * * * *

After being interrogated by Colleen, I sat at my desk with my hands folded on my desk in front of me. *Karma's a bitch*, I thought, *and that bitch's comin' at me wearing five-inch heels and carrying a nine millimeter!* Thoughts of all the wrong I'd done started to replay in my head, making me physically nauseous, from Bethany to Quick Rick and even my conspiracy to frame Elena. I had done a ton of bad, and now I was facing a whole lot of trouble.

The sound of my cell phone ringing snapped me out of my pained mental rewind. "This is Asia," I said, swallowing hard. I had a bad taste in my mouth and felt like I had a fever coming on.

"Meet me at the brownstone in thirty minutes," Parker commanded.

"Did Colleen talk to you?"

"Yes," he said. "Thirty minutes."

* * * * *

Standing in the empty living room, I watched Parker carefully. He stood looking out the window, appearing deep in thought.

"It took me six years to build that damn company up to what it is right now," he said. "Six fucking years, and now they want to take it from me. The board cast a unanimous vote that I should be relieved from my duties at G&L effective immediately," he said. "All that love and loyalty they had for me went straight out the damn window."

"It'll be alright," I said softly.

"She said if I confess, they'll cut me a deal," he rambled. "I don't need a damn deal. I'm only guilty of one thing."

I watched as he turned around and looked at me.

"I fell for you," he said.

"Regrets?" I asked.

"No regrets," he whispered, walking over to me. Pulling me into his arms, he exhaled. "Just consequences," he said.

Chapter 22

The first day of Parker's hearings, I was absent due to my own personal health. Every since returning from Tokyo, I had been feeling a little under the weather. At first, I thought it was jetlag, but after my body continued to ache after the first week, I knew it had to be something more. I tried to keep working through the aches and pains, but when I was hit with vomiting and diarrhea, I decided it was time for me to pay my doctor a visit.

After giving me a pregnancy test and basic STD scans, Dr. Thomas couldn't find a thing wrong with me. "We'll need to run additional tests," she said.

After her nurse, Sheila, took my blood, I informed them that I also wanted to give my consent for them to test for HIV. I had never been a praying woman, but my health scare and Parker's legal troubles drove me to my knees.

Parker's hearing was one of the most talked-about cases in history. Everyone wanted to know how a man so well respected and giving could now be standing trial for fraud and embezzlement. The charges brought against Parker were outstanding, and the evidence presented was crushing.

When it came time for me to take the stand, I felt like my heart would jump out my throat. As I sat on the witness stand, I looked at Parker. Even though the man was facing ten years in prison, he looked smooth and calm as ever. He gave me a slight wink of the eye as I began to answer the prosecutor's questions about my relationship with Parker, his spending, and my access to his credit card. I knew my testimony could help make or break Parker's case, and depending on how I played my cards, I could either be out the door or sitting on the throne.

Once all the evidence had been presented and every witness had testified, it took the jury less than eight hours to deliberate and bring back a guilty sentence. At the sound of the jury foreman's response, I immediately felt my breakfast coming back up. I rushed out of the courtroom, barely making it to the trashcan. It took six years for Parker to build his kingdom as CEO and less than forty-eight hours for him to be dethroned.

*****

I was sitting in the courthouse lobby with a bundle of wet paper towels pressed to my head when Dr. Thomas office called.

"Hello?"

"Asia?"

"Speaking."

"Asia, this is Sheila at Dr. Thomas's office."

"Hey, Sheila." I had a million thoughts running through my mind. I knew from history with Dr. Thomas that she never called when test results were negative.

"I wanted to let you know we got your test back," Sheila informed me. "Dr. Thomas would like for you to come in."

My heart began to skip a beat. I also knew getting called into the office was not a good thing. "Just tell me, Sheila" I said.

"Your HIV test was negative," she informed me.

I exhaled loudly into the phone. I was ecstatic!

"However, the blood pregnancy test was positive," she finished.

My excitement slightly fizzled. "What?" I stuttered.

"She wants you to come in for an ultrasound, just to be sure."

Chapter 23

Staring at the fuzzy black and white printout that Dr. Thomas had given me almost twenty-four hours earlier, I was still attempting to process what was happening. I had heard every word she had spoken: "Sometimes the urine test can give false negative results...what you thought was your period was probably just spotting…" and so on. "There's your baby," she'd said as she rolled the cold white probe along my belly. But even though I'd heard it and seen it, I still couldn't believe it; I didn't want to believe it.

If finding out I was pregnant wasn't bad enough, I was still attempting to deal with the fact that Parker was going to prison. I sat on the witness stand and told the truth that day—that Parker was an excellent boss who always tried to use integrity and honesty in every decision. I advised the jury that I had never seen Parker use the corporate credit card or any company funds for his own pleasure. Parker provided me with gifts and exposed me to luxury, but he did it all on his own dime. Granted, some of our escapades took place on company time, but as far as I knew, he used his own funding. When they asked me about close to $500,000 in misallocated funds, I didn't know a damn thing about what they were talking about.

When they got to the brunt of our relationship, I lied. I denied any and all wrongdoing. I had made Parker a promise way back in the beginning that I would never betray him, and I held true to that promise. Why? Loyalty—or maybe even gratefulness.

*****

After the trial, there were several transitions made at G&L. One included Jessica's and Jamel's resignations. Jessica's departure was based solely on the fact that Parker was no longer with the company. Jamel, however, resigned after pictures of him with another man—not Adam—surfaced on the Internet. There was a tiny voice telling me that Adam had something to do with everything, but I wasn't 100 percent sure.

Nathaniel left Elise and returned to G&L. The two of us built a strong relationship, and we were getting closer and closer every minute.

I walked into the office and smiled at the huge bouquet of yellow and white roses sitting on my desk, a gift from a new client. I loved the fact that I was gaining and building our clientele every day. Despite the fact that I was young and fairly new with the company, the clients accepted and respected me. Besides, I had already developed my own track record for landing major contracts. After all, I was the one who had brought home the monumental Ojima

Motors contract.

"Knock, knock," Nathaniel said, standing in the open doorway.

"Hey, Nate," I smiled.

"I have the Juicy Couture contract ready," he smiled. "All you have to do is sign off on it."

"That's what's up?" I smiled, giving him a high-five.

"How is baby boy?" he asked, rubbing my swollen belly.

"Two months and counting, Daddy," I smiled. "I can't wait to look down and see my toes again."

"I bet," he laughed. Giving me a quick peck on the lips, he looked at his watch. "I'll see you later, boo. I have a meeting."

"Love you," I said sincerely.

"I love you too."

Epilogue

Walking through the heavy metal doors, I smiled at the sight of Parker. The man was fine, even in prison whites. He had bulked up some in the short time he had been in the federal penitentiary, and I could only imagine how he was going to look after three years.

"It's good to see you, boo," I said, sitting down at the small table. "No hug? No love?"

Looking over at me, Parker shook his head. "How are you?"

"I'm good, but I would be even better if you would return a letter a time or two," I said, pouting. Since his incarceration, Parker had yet to write me back. The only reason he broke down and finally called me was because I told him I had a message from Asia.

"Jessica, this isn't a fucking vacation I'm on," he said. "I'm serving time. My career is over, and the woman I love—"

"The woman you love what?!" I spat. "She's got the money and the position and someone else to share it with. You are so damn gullible," I said. "I'm right here! I've always been right here!"

"I don't love you, Jessica," he said, staring at me. "I never kept that from you."

"Love is an emotion that can be developed," I said, "in due time."

"You can't force your emotions." Parker sighed. "It's either there or it's not."

"Fine. When you see how lonely it gets doing a four-year bid alone, let me know if it's there then. It could have been the two of us," I whined.

"Move on," he said, looking at me pathetically

"Fuck you, Parker," I said, laughing lightly. "Enjoy your time."

"Don't come back to see me again," he said, standing.

I watched him as he slowly began to walk away. "By the way, Parker," I said quickly. "I hear congratulations are in order. It seems you're going to be a daddy!"

My words stopped him in his tracks. He turned around and looked me dead in the eyes.

"That's right, Parker," I taunted. "Asia's pregnant, boo. It's a boy!"

*****

Slipping onto the elevator, I pressed the button for the fifth floor. .I still couldn't believe Parker was moping around over that bitch Asia. For six years, I was his everything. I was his lover, his secretary, his partner, and the one in whom he could confide. Whatever it was he needed, I provided it. Then she came along, and he lost his damn mind. Taking her on shopping sprees and putting her up in his brownstone? I'm a fan of anyone who donates to charity, but he fell in love with her. He gave her the position and the office that should have been mine. I refused to lose him, so I did what I had to do. I falsified documents and statements, stole cash, and played with the numbers. The receipts Colleen was provided were given to her by me. Why? It's quite simple. I can handle sharing a man's bed. Hell, I can even handle sharing his money, but I refuse to share his heart. You see, if I can't have his heart, then the next bitch can't either. I knew Parker loved her because he confessed to me that he did, so I made the phone call that day reporting inappropriate behavior at G&L, but I couldn't do it all alone. I needed help making it all look real. For that, I recruited a business acquaintance.

Carrying the large "It's a Boy" gift basket, I pushed through the glass doors. "Just the person I wanted to see," I said with a smile.

"Come right in, Jessica."

Following G&L's newest CEO into the office, I exhaled. "Still the same ol' office," I said, sitting the basket on the desk.

"Only from the outside."

"How have you been?" I asked, looking across the desk.

"Good. Tired, but good."

"I saw Parker today," I said, crossing my legs.

"How is he?"

"He looks good—real good."

"You still love him?"

"Our relationship is for life," I said confidentially. "He just doesn't realize it."

"You set him up, Jess. If that's love, I would hate to see your expression of hate."

"I would rather see him behind bars than with—"

Leaning forward, Nathaniel smiled. "Then with my fiancée?"

I was thinking, *That bitch*, but I wanted to show the man some respect for the woman he was planning to marry. "What do you two see in her?" I asked.

"If I remember correctly you've had better," I said, bluntly.

I was referring to my best friend, Antonia. Antonia and I had been the best of friends since college and were partially inseparable until she died during the birth of my goddaughter, Kaitlyn. When Antonia first introduced me to Nathaniel, I thought she was completely out of his league. Antonia was beautiful, intelligent, and classy. Granted, Nathaniel was educated and well dressed…really he's just a reformed thug. My opinion at the time was once a thug, always a thug. Nathaniel on the other hand proved to be a man about his business and his family. That's why I convinced Parker to hire Nathaniel in the first place. No one knew that Nathaniel and I were connected in our personal lives. That was Nathaniel's decision. He wanted to stand on his own two feet and show that he deserved to be at G&L because of his hard-work, not because one of his closest friends was Parker Bryant's assistant. The truth is, he could do his job and he could do it well but Parker was too damn cocky and pussy whipped to see it.

Now that things have taken a dramatic turn, I'm thankful that Nathaniel and I decided to keep our friendship a secret. If we hadn't, I'm sure Parker would have been suspicious of our little plan and things would have gone terribly wrong. Instead, things fell in place nicely. The day Asia stormed out of the office, I gave Nathaniel the address where he could find her with hope that the two of them would get cozy. Then I informed Parker that Nathaniel took Asia home to make sure she was alright. Parker, being the jealous man that he is, couldn't stay away. However, he was too little too late.

"There will never be another Antonia," Nathaniel said, softly. He looked away for a brief second then cleared his throat. It was obvious that he still missed my best friend terribly and a part of me felt like shit for bringing her name up.

"However, there is only one Asia," he said, shaking his head. His mood appeared to lighten at the mere mentioning of her name. *That bitch must have a pot of gold between her thighs*, I thought to myself.

"Again I ask what do you see in her?" I questioned sarcastically.

"Something you never could," Nathaniel laughed. "Something worth holding on to."

"If you say so," I sighed. "At least we both got what we want. I got Parker away from Asia," I said, smiling, "and you got the girl, baby boy, and finally the title of CEO."

"Any regrets?" I asked.

Shaking his head, Nathaniel smiled. "You know me better than that, Jess. I don't believe in regrets," he said. "Just consequences."

PRESENTS

Mz. Robinson

Married to His Lies

What We Won't Do for Love

Essence of a Bad Girl

&

Coming Soon…

The Lies We Tell for Love

George Sherman Hudson

Drama

Family Ties

Blocked In

&

Coming Soon…

City Lights

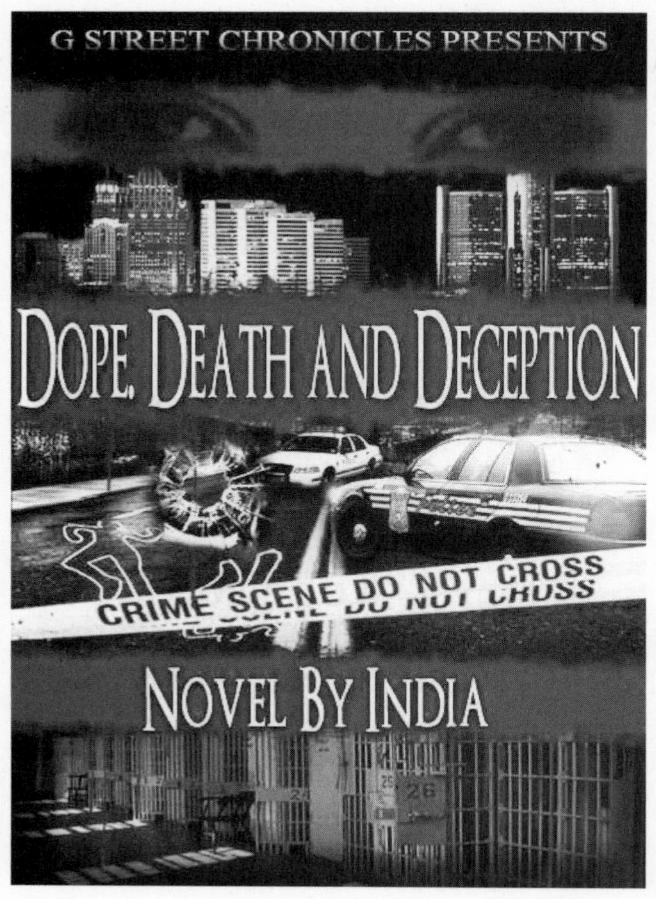
G STREET CHRONICLES PRESENTS
DOPE, DEATH AND DECEPTION
CRIME SCENE DO NOT CROSS
NOVEL BY INDIA

G STREET CHRONICLES PRESENTS
Blocked In
A Novel
GEORGE SHERMAN HUDSON

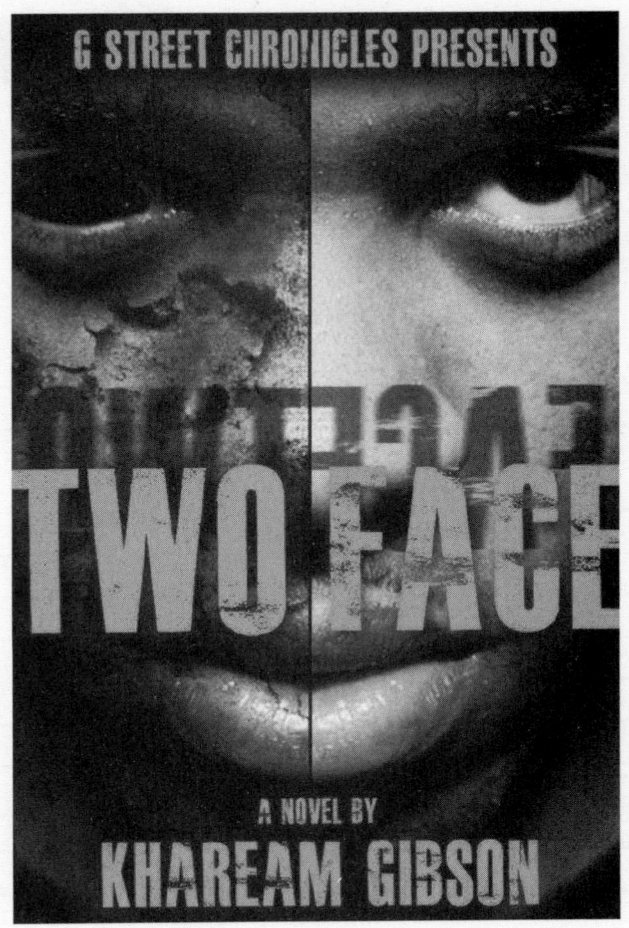
G STREET CHRONICLES PRESENTS
TWO FACE
A NOVEL BY
KHAREAM GIBSON

Name: ______________________

Address: ______________________

City/State: ______________________

Zip: ______________________

ALL BOOKS ARE $10 EACH

QTY	TITLE	PRICE
	Executive Mistress	
	City Lights	
	Dope, Death and Deception	
	Swagger	
	Drama	
	What We Won't Do for Love	
	Married to His Lies	
	Family Ties	
	Essence of a Bad Girl	
	Blocked In	
	Two Face	
	Never Satisfied	
	Pay Attention to the Red Flags	
	Shipping & Handling ($4 per book)	

TOTAL $ __________

To order online visit

www.gstreetchronicles.com

Send cashiers check or money order to:

G Street Chronicles

P.O. Box 490082 • College Park, GA 30349